Fix Your Small Appliances

Volume 1

by Jack Darr

HOWARD W. SAMS & CO., INC.
THE BOBBS-MERRILL CO., INC.
INDIANAPOLIS · KANSAS CITY · NEW YORK

FIRST EDITION

FIRST PRINTING—1974

International Standard Book Number: 0-672-21051-7
Library of Congress Catalog Card Number: 74-75275

Preface

This book covers small electrical appliances with heating elements. It is dedicated to the American Handyman—the traditional "tinkerer." He can fix most of the things around his home. This includes the many different makes and models of electrical appliances. All he needs is a little bit of information—how and why certain things are made, how to get them apart, and how to put them back together again after repairs are done. This information is what we'll try to provide in simple everyday language.

Electrical appliances are simple things. They may look complicated but they're not. An electric iron, for example, is nothing but a line cord, a heating element, a thermostat, and a switch. A mixer is just an electric motor, a little gearbox and a couple of beaters. Basically, all appliances are the same whether they're brand new or fairly old! They change very little. You'll find that some of the illustrations show older models, but if you'll check, you'll see that the new ones *work* exactly like the old models and can be fixed with the same methods.

You won't need a lot of expensive tools. Most of these appliances can be taken apart and put back together with only simple hand tools. Since all of these appliances are powered by electricity, I have included some of the basics on working with electricity. It's quite safe if you know what you're doing and use plain old common sense. Only time-tested, proven methods and tests are given, which have been worked out in actual servicing, in my own shop and home, on each of the units discussed in this book, and in Volume 2 of this series, which covers small electrical appliances with motors.

Keeping the small appliances going in your home can really build up your reputation with the family! In fact, after a little practice on your own appliances, you might even use this book to help you get started as a part-time or even full-time appliance repairman—always a welcome addition to a neighborhood. This can turn out to be quite profitable, too, with the literal "explosion" of small electrical appliances in this country! A skilled technician is always nice to have around.

Good luck to you.

JACK DARR

Contents

CHAPTER 1

DIAGNOSIS OF TROUBLE 7

Safety Precautions—Three-Wire Line Plugs, Cords, and Receptacles — Testing Techniques — Electrical Testing — Switch Cleaning and Replacement—Tools and Testing—Basic Electrical Tests—Line Cords, Plugs, and Attachments—Types of Cords Used—Wire Sizes—Plugs—Checking Line Cords for Wear and Aging—Cord Attachments and Strain Reliefs—Appliance Connectors—Fasteners and Wire Nuts

CHAPTER 2

HEATING ELEMENTS 39

Controlling the Heat—Testing and Repairing Heating Elements

CHAPTER 3

PORTABLE TABLE OVENS 46

Rotisseries

CHAPTER 4

ELECTRICAL COOKING APPLIANCES 57

Skillets — Servicing — Electric Griddles — Waffle Irons — Warming Plates

CHAPTER 5

ELECTRIC COOKERS AND COFFEE MAKERS 63

Dual-Heat Appliances—Coffee Makers—Replacement Heating Elements—Thermostats—Calibrated Thermostats

CHAPTER 6

ELECTRIC IRONS 75
    Steam Irons—Steam/Spray Irons—Repairs

CHAPTER 7

ELECTRIC TOASTERS 82
    The Self-Lowering Toasters—Servicing Automatic Toasters—
    Hot-Dog Cooker—Bottle Warmers—Vaporizers

CHAPTER 8

MODULAR APPLIANCES 96
    Percolator—Toaster—Combination Toaster and Table Oven—
    The Steam/Dry/Spray Iron

CHAPTER 9

PORTABLE ELECTRIC HEATERS 110
    Heater Repairs—Beauty-Care Appliances

CHAPTER 10

ELECTRIC BLANKETS AND HEATING PADS 122
    Blankets—Heating Pads

CHAPTER 11

LIGHTING AND CONTROLS 126
    Three-Way Lamps—Fluorescent Lights—Photoelectric Light
    Controls—Solid-State Light Dimmers

CHAPTER 12

MISCELLANEOUS REPAIR TECHNIQUES 138
    Repairing Broken Appliance Cases—Plastic Cases—Repairing
    the Tough Ones—Broken Studs—Bolts, Nuts, and Screws

CHAPTER 13

APPLIANCE SERVICING 145
    Timesaving Tools — Power Tools — Chemical Aids — When
    Chemicals Won't Work—Parts Procurement

APPENDIX

GLOSSARY 155

INDEX 159

Diagnosis of Trouble

On getting a complaint that a certain appliance is not working, the first thing we must do is to find out why. If we use a logical sequence of tests based on the knowledge of how the appliance works, we can find the trouble and fix it quickly. Random "poking around" can take a lot of time, and you'll find the trouble only by accident. The basic method of fixing any kind of electrical apparatus begins with the use of the logical sequence method of testing. All machines are inherently logical, and if we don't use logic when working on them, we are wasting time. The first step in the logical sequence of tests for this kind of apparatus is determining if there is any electrical power to the unit; we must have electrical power before the unit can work at all. Second, we must find out just which part is not working, such as the motor, heating element, etc. Third, we must see if it can be fixed or if we will have to replace it. That's all there is to this method.

Find out the nature of the complaint—completely dead, works intermittently, makes funny noises, etc. From here, we can go on to testing one particular part and save a lot of time. For example, if the complaint is "rattles," we can skip one step in the procedure—if it rattles, it is at least trying to work and it does have power; we can skip the step that calls for checking the line cord, plug, etc., and start looking for loose screws or parts.

SAFETY PRECAUTIONS

The power supply to your home is 117-volt, 60-hertz alternating current, and it can inflict serious injury or even death if you are careless. You must know how to handle it, what to do, and, above all, what *not* to do. Learn the rules and obey them at all times. Train yourself in safe working methods, and most important, never get careless or contemptuous of electricity—this can be fatal. The professional electrician seems to handle electrical wires with carelessness, but this is not true. He is trained to take these safety precautions automatically.

There are a very few simple rules that you must follow:

1. *Never touch a bare wire* if the appliance is plugged into an electrical outlet. You can get a shock by touching the wires; the circuit is completed through your body. If you are wearing leather-soled shoes and standing on bare earth or a cement floor, you are grounded. The "service wires" from the transformer go to your house service center, where the fuses or circuit breakers protect your wiring against shorts. One side of the service line is always grounded, but the other side has 117-volts alternating current *with respect to ground* at all times. You can make voltage tests to find out which one is hot. However, when you are *working* on any kind of electrical equipment, be very sure that all power is *off* by pulling the plug.

2. *Never* work on an appliance that is plugged in. You can make certain tests, as we said, but when you change parts, make connections, disconnect wiring, etc., make sure that the line plug is pulled out of the wall outlet and lying on the bench or table where you can see it.

3. For the safety of the one who will use this appliance, be *very* sure that there are no short circuits from the ac wiring to the metal case of the appliance. If the metal case of a toaster and the sink faucet are touched at the same time, a dangerous or fatal shock can be obtained, since water piping is a perfect ground.

When an appliance is disassembled, note very carefully how the wire connections are made, and be sure that they are put back so that there will never be any possibility of a bare wire getting in contact with any other part of the appliance. After completing the repairs, check for voltage between the case of the appliance and a water pipe. Pull the line plug, reverse it, and recheck. If your test lamp does not light in either position, it will indicate proper wiring of the line cord. There is always the chance of an accidental short or leakage between the internal wiring and the case. This can be an internal leakage in the motor windings, etc. It can be a "dead short" or just a leakage, which can cause the complaint of "it tingles whenever I touch it." Investigate this immediately; a *tingle* means a small leakage, but this can turn into a short circuit at any time. Fig. 1-1 shows a test lamp which can be used to make this test. Use well-insulated clips, and never connect this with power on!

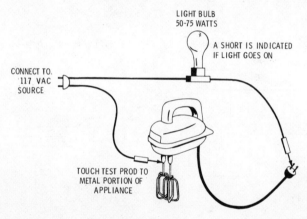

LIGHT BULB
50-75 WATTS

A SHORT IS INDICATED
IF LIGHT GOES ON

CONNECT TO.
117 VAC
SOURCE

TOUCH TEST PROD TO
METAL PORTION OF
APPLIANCE

Fig. 1-1. Checking for a short between the motor or appliance frame and the ac line. Connect one prod to the line cord and the other to the frame of the appliance. The light will go on if there is a short between the ac line and the appliance frame.

One item that must always be checked very carefully before you consider an appliance fully repaired is accidental grounding of the windings to the motor or appliance frame. Such an oversight could cause a serious or even fatal shock, because most appliances are used on or near sinks, within easy reach of well-grounded water pipes. A small tester can be assembled from a 50-watt lamp, a socket, and a pair of wires with test prods, as shown in Fig. 1-1. Connect one prod to the line cord and the other to the frame of the appliance. The light will go on if there is a ground (short) between the ac line and the frame of the motor or appliance.

THREE-WIRE LINE PLUGS, CORDS, AND RECEPTACLES

The latest *standard* for safety in home electrical appliances is called the *three-wire* line cord. These have three conductors and a special three-prong plug; Fig. 1-2 shows one of these.

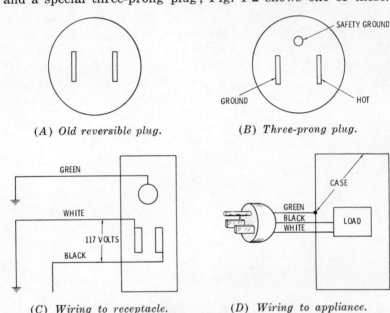

(A) *Old reversible plug.*   (B) *Three-prong plug.*

(C) *Wiring to receptacle.*   (D) *Wiring to appliance.*

Fig. 1-2. Typical three-wire line plugs, cord, and receptacle. The flat prongs are the same as the older types. The round pin is a "safety ground."

The flat prongs are the same as the older types, and the round pin is a *safety ground.* (To remember this, think of "round for ground.") In the line cords you'll find a black wire, a white wire, and a green wire. (Incidentally, the green wire is the only one in the National Fire Underwriter's Code that is coded a specific *color.*) In the standard-code-wired 117-volt ac home circuits, black wires should always be *hot*, and white wires *ground*. These cords and plugs require a special three-pin receptacle and a three-wire supply. In the *current-carrying* circuits supplying power to the appliance, the black wire is hot and the white wire is ground. The green wire must *never* be used in the current-carrying circuits. Instead, it should be connected to a separate ground at the service center (fuse or circuit-breaker box).

Inside the appliance itself, the green wire must be connected to the metal case and to all exposed metal parts. This is to prevent danger should there be a short circuit from the hot wire to the case. If a hot wire contacts the grounded case, it will blow the fuse or trip the circuit breaker; that's all it's supposed to do! If any appliance instantly blows the fuse or trips the circuit breaker when it's plugged in, take it apart and find the short circuit.

You can add this type of *safety wire* to older appliances, but your home must be wired with the three-wire supply, the special-type outlets, and the safety ground must be added. Do *not* replace the older two-wire outlets with the three-wire type. This might lead someone to believe that he is protected against shock when he is not.

Later, we'll discuss checking line cords for normal wear, insulation for aging signs, connections for faulty operation, etc. You can spot these potential hazards easily and repair them before they endanger someone. Line cords are a common cause of trouble since they are stepped on, crushed, bent, and twisted.

TESTING TECHNIQUES

Check the line cord for signs of bad insulation, and check the plug for loose connections. If the appliance does not work, make sure that the plug fits tightly in the wall outlet, and check to make sure that the outlet itself is working properly. A common trouble with line cords is a broken wire inside the insulation near the plug. Hold the plug with one hand and bend the wire back and forth; if the appliance suddenly starts to work, cut off the cord about 6 inches from the plug and install a new plug.

If the cord seems to be in operating condition, pull the plug and open the case of the appliance so that you can get at the other end of the cord. If the ends are fastened with wire nuts, take these off. Make sure that the wires are not touching each other or any part of the appliance. Plug it in again, and check it with a light bulb between the exposed ends to make certain that you're getting power up to that point. If you do, then the cord is definitely in good shape, and the trouble is in the appliance itself.

ELECTRICAL TESTING

We will need to check for electrical power in all appliances, and the simplest way to do this is to check for voltage. You can get small, imported, ac voltmeters for less than $10 each, but many professional men use a simple "test lamp" which costs even less. Fig. 1-3 shows the two most common types of test

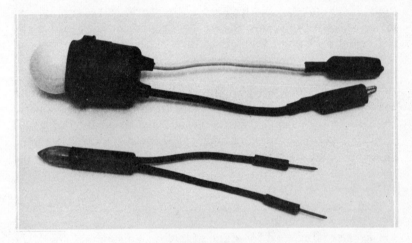

Fig. 1-3. Two common-type test lamps. The top one is a 7-watt incandescent lamp in a weatherproof socket. The bottom one is a tiny neon bulb which has a series resistor inside a plastic housing.

lamps. At the top is an incandescent lamp in a weatherproof socket. The socket is covered with soft rubber and has flexible wire leads. Attach a pair of insulated test clips to these and put in a small 7-watt lamp, and you will be ready to go. To check for the presence of voltage across any circuit, just clip one lead to each side, and if the lamp lights, voltage is present.

Also shown is a special neon voltage tester, sold in auto supply stores, radio stores, etc. A tiny neon bulb has a plastic housing and flexible leads with test tips. A series resistor is used inside the housing to make the lamp operate on 117 volts or even on 220 volts for short periods. The lamp will glow on 117 volts and will glow much brighter on 220 volts. There are advantages and disadvantages, as will be explained, but this type of test lamp is not expensive and should be included in your test equipment.

Using the Test Lamps

The 7-watt test lamp can be used for testing line cords, switches, and similar circuits. For example, if you want to check a line cord for a possible intermittent condition, hook the test lamp to the ends of the cord inside the appliance. Plug it in and turn the switch on. The lamp should light. Now, hold the line cord and shake it back and forth. Move it, pull it, and watch the lamp. If there are any intermittent connections, the lamp will go off and on or flicker. To check a switch, hook the lamp from one side of the line to the "load" side of the switch (see Fig. 1-4) so that the current has to flow through the switch. If you wish, you can use a most useful electrical test here—the "simulated load." For example, if you are checking small appliances (about 35–40 watts) disconnect the appliance and put a 50-watt lamp in the tester. By hooking this across the line, you will draw the same amount of current as the appliance. You can check this by looking at the rating plate on the case; it will give the normal wattage drawn.

Now, turn the switch on and see if it operates every time. If it is dirty or making intermittent contact, the lamp will flicker or even refuse to light at all. The neon tester can be used for this, but, because of its sensitivity, it is not as reliable as the load test. Even if the switch is dirty, the neon lamp will

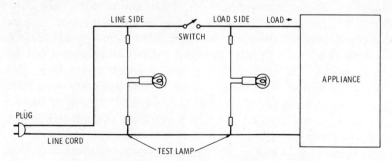

Fig. 1-4. Checking an appliance switch with a test lamp.

light because it draws very little current. You can use this test for loads up to about 150 watts. For large heating-element appliances, such as space heaters, etc., which can pull up to 1000 watts, it is not practical. The best way is to use the heating element itself as the load.

The sensitivity of the neon tester can be put to good use. For example, to find out whether a certain circuit is grounded or not, hold one of the test tips in your hand, and touch the *other one* to the circuit. If there is any voltage present, the lamp will glow. The current here passes through your body, but it is so very small that you cannot feel it. This test is especially useful when one is working on house wiring; if you check both sides of the line and do not get a glow, then there is no voltage. The small tips of the test leads can be used to find out if there is any voltage at a wall outlet. Push them into the slots, and if there is voltage present, the lamp will light up brightly. If you get no light on this test, then check the fuses or circuit breaker. You must have voltage at the outlet before you can make any further tests.

Another "dirty switch" test can be made with the neon lamp. Plug in the appliance, turn it *on,* and then touch the test tips directly across the switch itself. Of course, when the switch is turned *on,* it should be a complete "short circuit." However, if it is dirty or not making contact properly, there will be a small voltage drop across the switch. If the lamp flickers when across a closed (on) switch, the switch is probably very dirty and should be replaced.

Testing for Grounds

As we said, there is one very important test that must be made on *all* appliances when you finish the repair. This is to find out if the case of the unit is shorted to the ac line. If you have been careful, this will not happen, but never take chances with electricity—find out by making positive checks. Plug in the appliance and turn it on, and then touch one side of the little neon tester to the case. Hook a long piece of wire to a grounded object and touch the other tip of the neon tester to this, keeping both hands clear. If you have a ground inside the case, the lamp will glow.

If it passes this test, pull the plug, turn it halfway over and put it back. Now repeat the test. Remember, we said that one side of the ac line is hot at all times and the other is always grounded. So this second test will catch any kind of one-sided ground that might be present. Incidentally, on larger appliances, such as the washer, dryer, etc., you can make it perfectly safe by running an *extra* ground wire from the frame of the unit to a water pipe. Fasten one end of the ground wire to a bolt, and clamp the other to the cold-water pipe. If the unit does short out, you will blow the fuse but no one will be injured.

SWITCH CLEANING AND REPLACEMENT

A faulty switch is one of the most common causes of appliance trouble. In many appliances it is the only moving part. As a switch is used, its contacts gradually get dirty or burned from arcing. Eventually the time comes when the contacts simply will not close. The tests previously given will show this. If the switch is intermittent, it can often be cleaned and made to work for a while longer. A spray cleaner, of the kind used in radio-television shops, can help if it is sprayed directly inside the switch.

Replacement switches can be found at appliance dealers. If the switch is a standard on-off type, it will be easy to find. If it is a special-type switch, you will probably have to get an exact-duplicate replacement from the dealer carrying that line of appliances. Take along the make and model number of the appliance, any part numbers that might be on the switch itself, or, preferably, the old switch. Before disconnecting a switch of the more complicated type with more than two wires, make a sketch of the wires, the switch, and include the wire colors, or put little paper tags on each wire. This will eliminate any chance for mistakes in connecting the new switch.

TOOLS AND TESTING

Any kind of repair job is easier if you have the right tools. To work on electrical appliances, you will not need a lot of expensive tools, but it will be much simpler if you have the right ones. You will find screws set down in holes, hard-to-get-at bolts, and such things. With the proper tools, they are simple to handle, but without them life can get complicated. You can find these tools at hardware stores, radio supply houses, and such places. Fig. 1-5 shows the essential tool kit: a 6-inch standard screwdriver, a Phillips screwdriver, a pair of 6-inch gaspliers, a 4-inch adjustable wrench, and a pocketknife. With these tools you can take apart and reassemble almost all common home appliances. Fig. 1-6 shows some helpful special tools; at the right is a set of nutdrivers or socket wrenches, from $\frac{1}{8}$ inch up to $\frac{1}{2}$ inch in steps of $\frac{1}{32}$ inch. An extra handle is provided to give better grip on the small handles. Next to these are two screwholding-type screwdrivers, very handy for getting screws and bolts started in tight places. At left is a three-way tap with a plastic handle, with the three most common sizes of thread. This is useful for restoring damaged threads in screw holes or for threading oversize holes to the next larger size of screw.

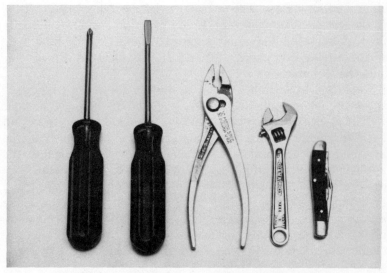

Fig. 1-5. The essential tools needed in appliance repair.

Fig. 1-7 shows a handy tool; this is a *crimping tool,* with some samples of the terminals used with it also illustrated. By using these terminals, you can put new connections on any wire without having to solder them. In some cases, this is essential because you cannot solder terminals to the ends of a heating element. Solder will not stick to heater wire, and the

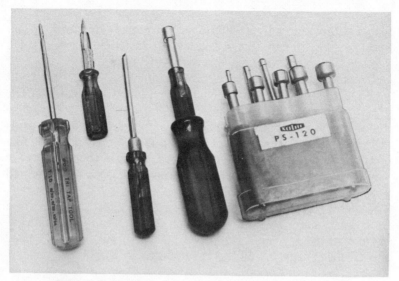

Fig. 1-6. Special tools used in making the repair job easier.

wire will operate hotter than the melting point of solder, so a *solderless* terminal is necessary. This is also very handy for repairing wiring in your automobile, since most modern cars use this type of wiring terminal.

Fig. 1-8 shows the standard equipment for repairing wiring: a soldering gun, long-nose and cutting pliers, and, of course, the pocketknife. There are many other tools which can be added to your tool kit as the need arises, e.g., a small 6- to 8-inch flat mill file, a small punch which can be a standard *nail set*, and a hammer. You will find some appliances which have been riveted together. The only way to take these apart is to file off the head of the rivet and use a punch to knock the rest of the rivet out. You can replace these by using pop rivets,

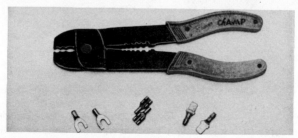

Fig. 1-7. A terminal crimping tool and some of the various terminals.

also available at radio and auto supply stores. However, if you want to make the appliance easier to disassemble the next time, replace the rivets with No. 6 screws with nuts.

Use lockwashers under all nuts, and they will stay tight much longer. In cases where you cannot get to the inside of the unit to put on a nut, use a *self-tapping* or *metal* screw. The metal screw cuts its own threads as it is installed, and it is found in a great many sheet metal applications today. If one of the metal screws has been stripped out, use the next larger size; for instance, if the original screw was a No. 4 and it will not hold because the hole has been enlarged, use a No. 6 screw. The metal screws come with standard and Phillips heads, and in a great many applications (such as auto radios), they are hexagonal-head ¼-inch types. To get these out, you will need the ¼-inch nutdriver of the type shown in Fig. 1-6.

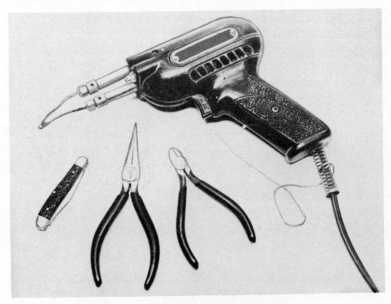

Fig. 1-8. Tools necessary for wire repair.

BASIC ELECTRICAL TESTS

There are two kinds of defects in electrical circuits. One is a "short circuit" where the two wires touch each other. This blows a fuse or trips a circuit breaker. (Or it should! If it doesn't, you're bucking for a fire!) The second is an "open circuit" which simply means that a wire has broken somewhere. Nothing works. You can check for either type with a small ohmmeter. Let's see how.

Continuity

Every electrical circuit must have "continuity." This means that there must be a continuous path for the current. This path starts at one side of the ac line plug, goes through the line cord (one wire), through the switch, through the load, then back through the other wire of the line cord to the ac line plug. If this path has a break in it anywhere, the circuit is open and no current can flow. Fig. 1-9A illustrates a simple circuit.

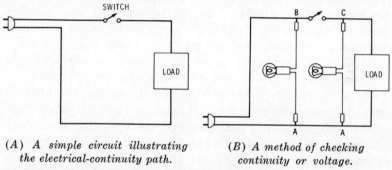

(A) A simple circuit illustrating the electrical-continuity path.

(B) A method of checking continuity or voltage.

Fig. 1-9. These circuits illustrate the electrical-continuity path and a method of checking for continuity.

You can make continuity tests with either one of the test lamps, as shown in Fig. 1-9B. Connect the line plug to the outlet, and check to see if you get a glow between "A" and "B." If so, you have power to this point. Close the switch and check from "A" to "C." If the test lamp glows here, you have power *across* the load. If the load is open, it won't work. For example, if this is a heating element and you read voltage across it but it doesn't get hot, you know it is open.

Testing with the Ohmmeter

You can check continuity with the ohmmeter without having power applied to the circuit. An ohmmeter is a small instrument with a built-in battery; it supplies its own power for continuity testing. Line cords and similar connectors should measure very low resistance, if any. The same reading can be obtained if you short the ohmmeter prods together. Heating elements will show comparatively low resistance. For a rule of thumb, the *lower* the resistance of a heating element, the greater its wattage (heat). Although various units will show differing amounts of resistance, with a little practice you'll learn what to expect on each different kind of load.

The ohmmeter is especially handy for locating short circuits. (CAUTION: *When making any test with an ohmmeter, be sure that all power is disconnected from the appliance!*) That's why we recommend making most of these tests across the prongs of the ac line plug. If you're connected to the prongs of the plug, the unit can't be plugged in. To check for a short, clip the ohmmeter across the two flat prongs of the line plug. Turn the switch of the appliance on. If the unit has been blowing fuses the instant it's plugged in, you'll probably see a 0-ohms reading. This is the same reading that you get when you short the test clips together. Incidentally, it is a good idea to zero the ohmmeter before making any resistance tests. It tells you that the ohmmeter is *working*. Adjust the OHMS ZERO knob so that the needle sits over the "O" mark on the OHMS scale.

The 0-ohms reading indicates that there is, indeed, a short somewhere in the circuit. To find out which part has the short, disconnect something. Let's say that we have a line cord, a switch, and a heating element with a normal resistance of 50

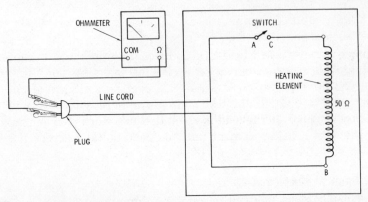

Fig. 1-10. Troubleshooting with ohmmeter. To check for a short circuit, connect the ohmmeter leads to the prongs of the line plug and disconnect the line cord at point "A." If the ohmmeter still reads 0 ohms, the short is in the line cord.

ohms. Fig. 1-10 shows the schematic diagram. To find out which part of the electrical circuit is bad, disconnect parts and check them one at a time. Here, we disconnect the line cord at point "A." Now, check the ohmmeter reading (which should still be connected to the prongs of the plug). If this still shows a 0-ohms reading, the short is in the line cord itself. To be certain, leave the line cord disconnected at "A" and take a reading from "B" to the "A" terminal of the switch. If this shows the normal 50 ohms with the switch closed, you've found the trouble. Replace the line cord. The same basic method can be used to check for shorts in the switch, heating element, or anything else.

Open circuits can be located with the same method. Clip one lead of the ohmmeter to either one of the prongs of the line plug. Now, check the inside end and see if you get a 0-ohms reading on one wire. If so, that's the one you're connected to at the plug, and this wire is good. Go on through the switch, heating element, etc., and through the other side of the line cord. If you get a reading at "B" but no reading at all on the other prong of the line plug, the line cord is open. Check the cord to see if the insulation shows any signs of breaks or cracking (or fraying on braid-covered types). If so, replace the whole line cord and plug.

LINE CORDS, PLUGS, AND ATTACHMENTS

Every electrical appliance has a line cord. (What about the cordless ones? They do too—on the recharging unit!) By far the most common job on appliances is replacement of the line cord. Constant flexing, aging, and abuse wear them out very quickly. Develop a habit of keeping an eye on the condition of the line cords on *all* of your appliances; it pays. Broken insulation on a cord can cause fire, shock, etc.

TYPES OF CORDS USED

Each appliance uses a line cord selected for its particular service. Small appliances employ the common zip cord used on tv sets and radios. Others use a slightly heavier jacketed wire; the heaviest of all is the asbestos-insulated wire for electric irons and heaters. No matter what the type, though, it must be flexible. So from now on, whenever any line cord is mentioned, remember that it is *always* stranded wire. (The only solid wires used in appliances are in heating elements and similar applications.)

POSJ Cord

POSJ is the Underwriter's Code classification for zip cord. It is rubber- or plastic-insulated (Fig. 1-11) and has a groove down the center for easy separation—hence the name, zip cord. Each conductor is wrapped with a fiber *lay* inside the insulation. Zip, or POSJ, cord is available in sizes from No. 18 (the smallest) up to about No. 10. The No. 18 gauge at the left in

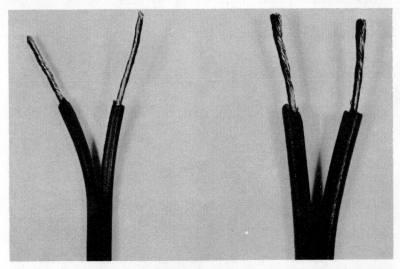

Fig. 1-11. Zip cord, more correctly known as POSJ (an underwriter's code designation), is used for many appliances. The No. 18 gauge at the left is the more common; it is employed on appliances requiring relatively small loads. At the right is a section of No. 16 gauge for heavier-load applications. Notice the "groove" down the center, for easy separation of the conductors.

Fig. 1-11 is the more common; it is employed on appliances requiring relatively small loads. At the right in Fig. 1-11 is a section of No. 16 gauge for heavier-load applications.

SV Cord

SV cord is a jacketed cable consisting of two rubber-insulated wires over a fiber lay, with an additional fiber filler be-

Fig. 1-12. SV cord is a jacketed cable used for heavy-duty service. It consists of two stranded conductors, each one insulated with rubber. A fiber "filler" is used between the wires, and a rubber or plastic jacket covers the entire assembly.

tween them. The outer covering consists of a heavy rubber or plastic jacket for added protection (Fig. 1-12).

Heater Cord

Heater cord should always be used on electric irons, waffle irons, and any other appliance whose heating elements draw more than 500 watts. (An electric iron consumes one kilowatt, as do waffle irons and grilles.) Each wire has a fiber wrap and rubber insulation, and is individually wrapped with stranded asbestos fibers. An extra fiber or asbestos filler is placed around both wires, and the outer covering is a tightly woven braided jacket (Fig. 1-13).

Three-Wire Cable

Three-wire cable is a rubber-jacketed wire often used on drills and similar tools. It is like the SV cord but has an additional wire which is used as a grounding conductor (Fig. 1-14). This third wire, always coded green, is fastened to the frame of the appliance; the other end goes to a third prong on a special line plug or to a pigtail coming out of the cable just above the plug. (The pigtail should be connected to a good ground.) Incidentally, this type of cord can be installed on any electrical appliance. It should always be employed where the user may have to stand on damp or conductive material such as cement floors, earth, etc. These plugs must be used with

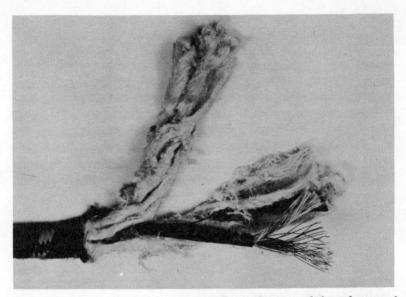

Fig. 1-13. Heater cord such as this usually employs stranded conductors of about No. 14 or 12 gauge. These are insulated with rubber and wrapped with asbestos fibers. The entire assembly is then covered with a stout braided jacket.

Fig. 1-14. This three-wire cable is similar to the SV cord in Fig. 2-2, but has an extra conductor (always coded green). This conductor is connected to the frame of the appliance, in order to ground it for safety and thereby eliminate a possible shock hazard to the user.

the correct type of outlet and wiring. The safety ground must be connected to the outlet.

WIRE SIZES

Line cords must be able to carry the normal current load without heating up and causing a loss of power. Table 1-1 shows the current-carrying capacity of standard wire sizes. Somewhere on every appliance is a rating plate showing the total wattage required. From $W = EI$ we get $I = W \div E$, from which we can find the current. This need not be a precise figure. For example, an appliance drawing 200 watts at 117 volts would have a current of about 2 amperes. Note that any of the types of No. 18 wire listed in Table 1-1 will handle this current with an adequate safety factor. Remember, these wires are stranded and some of the strands will eventually break from the continual flexing. If the wire is large enough, it will still have enough strands left to hold up for quite a while; but wire that is too small will overheat and present a definite fire hazard. In making any electrical repairs—especially appliance repairs—the utmost in safety should be your major objective;

Table 1-1. Capacity of Flexible Cord (in Amperes)

Size AWG	Rubber Types PO, C, PD, P, PW, K, E, EO Thermoplastic Type ET	Rubber Types S, SO, SRD, SJ, SJO, SV, SP Thermoplastic Types ST, SRDT, SJT, SVT, SPT	Types AFS, AFSJ, HC, HPD, HSJ, HS, HPN	Types AVPO, AVPD	Cotton Types CFC* CFPO* CFPD* Asbestos Types AFC* AFPO* AFPD*
18	5	7	10	17	6
17	—	—	12	—	—
16	7	10	15	22	8
15	—	—	17	—	—
14	15	15	20	28	17
12	20	20	30	36	23
10	25	25	35	47	28
8	35	35	—	—	—
6	45	45	—	—	—
4	60	60	—	—	—
2	80	—	—	—	—

*These types are used almost exclusively in fixtures where they are exposed to high temperatures, and ampre ratings are assigned accordingly.

Table 1-2. Types of Line Cord Wire Used for Different Classes of Service

Trade Name	Type Letter	Size AWG	No. of Conductors	Insulation	Outer Covering	Use
Asbestos-Covered, Heat-Resistant Cord	AFC		2 or 3	Impregnated Asbestos	None	Pendant, Dry Places, Not Hard Usage
	AFPO	18-10	2		Cotton, Rayon or Saturated Asbestos	
	AFPD		2 or 3			
Cotton-Covered, Heat-Resistant Cord	CFC		2 or 3	Impregnated Cotton	None	Pendant, Dry Places, Not Hard Usage
	CFPO	18-10	2		Cotton or Rayon	
	CFPD		2 or 3			
All-Rubber Parallel Cord	SP-1	18		Rubber	Rubber	Pendant or Portable, Damp Places, Not Hard Usage
	SP-2	18-16	2			Refrigerators or Room Air Conditioners
	SP-3	18-12		Rubber	Rubber	
All-Plastic Parallel Cord	SPT-1	18		Thermoplastic	Thermoplastic	Pendant or Portable, Damp Places, Not Hard Usage
	SPT-2	18-16	2			Refrigerators or Room Air Conditioners
	SPT-3	18-12	2	Thermoplastic	Thermoplastic	
Lamp Cord	C	18-10	2 or more	Rubber	None	Pendant or Portable, Dry Places, Not Hard Usage

Cord Type	Designation	AWG	Conductors	Insulation	Covering	Usage
Twisted, Portable Cord	PD	18-10	2 or more	Rubber	Cotton or Rayon	Pendant or Portable, Dry Places, Not Hard Usage
Reinforced Cord	P-1	18	2 or more	Rubber	Cotton over Rubber Filler	Pendant or Portable, Dry Places, Not Hard Usage
	P-2	18-16				
	P	18-10				Hard Usage
Moisture-Proof, Reinforced Cord	PW-1	18	2 or more	Rubber	Cotton, Moisture-Resistant Finish over Rubber Filler	Pendant or Portable, Damp Places, Not Hard Usage
	PW-2	18-16				
	PW	18-10				Hard Usage
Braided, Heavy-Duty Cord	K	18-10	2 or more	Rubber	Two Cotton, Moisture-Resistant Finish	Pendant or Portable, Damp Places, Hard Usage
Vacuum Cleaner Cord	SV	18	2	Rubber	Rubber	Pendant or Portable, Damp Places, Not Hard Usage
	SVT			Thermoplastic	Thermoplastic	
Junior-Hard-Service Cord	SJ	18-16	2, 3, or 4	Rubber	Rubber	Pendant or Portable, Damp Places, Hard Usage
	SJO			Rubber	Oil-Resistant Compound	
	SJT			Thermoplastic or Rubber	Thermoplastic	

Table 1-2. Types of Line Cord Wire Used for Different Classes of Service—cont

Trade Name	Type Letter	Size AWG	No. of Conductors	Insulation	Outer Covering	Use
Hard-Service Cord	S				Rubber	Pendant or Portable, Damp Places, Extra Hard Usage
	SO	18-10	2 or more	Rubber	Oil-Resistant Compound	
	ST			Thermoplastic or Rubber	Thermoplastic	
Rubber-Jacketed, Heat-Resistant Cord	AFSJ	18-16	2 or 3	Impregnated Asbestos	Rubber	Damp Places, Portable Heaters
	AFS	18-16-14				
Heater Cord	HC	18-12		Rubber & Asbestos	None	Dry Places, Portable Heaters
	HPD		2, 3, or 4		Cotton or Rayon	
Rubber-Jacketed Heater Cord	HSJ	18-16	2, 3, or 4	Rubber & Asbestos	Cotton and Rubber	Damp Places, Portable Heaters
Jacketed Heater Cord	HS	14-12	2, 3, or 4	Rubber & Asbestos	Cotton and Rubber or Neoprene	Damp Places, Portable Heaters
All-Neoprene Heater Cord	HPN	18-16	2	Neoprene	Neoprene	Damp Places, Portable Heaters
Heat- & Moisture-Resistant Cord	AVPO	18-10	2	Asbestos and Var. Cam.	Asbestos, Flame-Resistant Moisture-Resistant	Pendant or Portable, Damp Places, Not Hard Usage
	AVPD		2 or 3			

the appliances will be used by women and children, most of whom are a little short on knowledge of electricity and safety precautions. Table 1-2 shows the many different types of wire used for appliances.

Many new appliances have small line cords; some are too small, especially for high-current units like heaters, hair dryers, etc. Check these in use; if the line cord gets *hot*, it isn't big enough. Take it off and replace it with a cord having larger wire! No line cord should be even warm, for safety's sake.

PLUGS

Quite a few types of plugs are used on appliances—some for connecting to the power source, and others for connection to the appliance itself. Almost all original-equipment cords are terminated in a molded plastic plug; the small one on a tv line cord is a good example (Fig. 1-15).

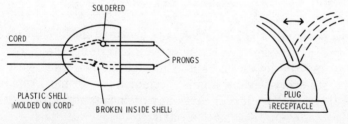

(A) *Where break usually occurs.*   (B) *Method of checking.*

Fig. 1-15. Power cords often cause trouble by opening or shorting at the plug.

The most frequent trouble is a broken wire inside the plug, as shown in Fig. 1-15A. This is due to constant flexing of the wire, and it can be hard to find unless you're watching for it. Whenever repairing *any* appliance using such a plug, check by bending the wire back and forth (Fig. 1-15B) with the appliance turned on, and watch for signs of intermittent contact. If trouble shows up, clip off the plug and replace it.

There are several choices here: probably the best for all-around replacement is the rubber-shell type with removable prongs. A group of appliance replacement plugs is shown in Fig. 1-16. At the lower left is a plastic plug; the end of the wire is slipped into the lower part and the prongs pushed together.

Fig. 1-16. Replacement plugs are available in a variety of types. Some typical examples are shown above.

Spikes penetrate the insulation, and the shell holds it in place. The two at the top are connected by attaching the wires to screws. At the lower right is a molded rubber plug with an insert; it is very durable and is recommended for most replacement work because it will carry any of the standard household appliances, even 1-kilowatt electric irons.

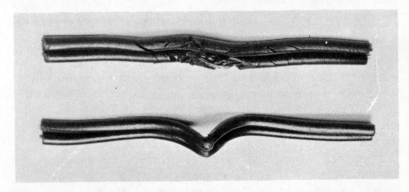

Fig. 1-17. Line cords can become dangerous. The ones above are often referred to as "The Fireman's Friend," and when in this condition, should be replaced rather than repaired.

CHECKING LINE CORDS FOR WEAR AND AGING

Whenever any electrical appliance is checked, the line cord should be inspected very carefully. Worn or aged insulation can create a fire hazard.

Years ago, line cords were made of reclaimed rubber or the early synthetics, and they understandably weren't too good! These cords caused more than their share of trouble when placed near a window because direct sunlight played havoc with them. In later years, improved synthetics have made the line cords quite durable—but watch out for the older ones!

The quickest insulation test is to bend the cord sharply between the fingers. If the surface shows tiny cracks or if it crumbles off entirely (Fig. 1-17), replace the cord. Look for

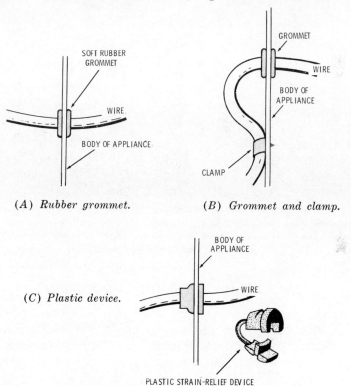

(A) *Rubber grommet.*   (B) *Grommet and clamp.*

(C) *Plastic device.*

Fig. 1-18. Examples of various strain-relieving methods. Strain relievers should be used where the line cord goes into the appliance to keep any strain off the electrical connections inside.

most troubles to occur at the ends, where the greatest amount of flexing occurs. At times the cord will be worn only at the ends. If it won't make the cord too short, clip out the bad parts and replace the plug. Check first, though, or you may get into trouble! I cut off about 6 inches of a line cord one day only to receive a severe tongue lashing the next! It seems the cord *had been* just long enough to put the mixer where the lady wanted it. She kept after me until I installed a new cord.

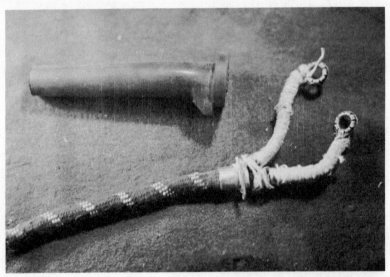

Fig. 1-19. An iron cord ready for installation. Notice the small metal clamp where the wires divide; this is used to keep the strain off the electrical connections. The soft rubber sleeve shown in the photo prevents the cord from being bent and kinked too sharply.

CORD ATTACHMENTS AND STRAIN RELIEFS

At the point where the line cord goes into the appliance, there should always be a firm anchorage to keep any strain off the electrical connections. Devices used for this purpose are called *strain reliefs,* and several are shown in Fig. 1-18. In Fig. 1-18A the power cord is passed through a rubber grommet to provide further protection, or a clamp like that shown in Fig. 1-18B may be used. Fig. 1-18C shows a plastic strain-relief device in two sections, one for each side of the cord.

When assembled, it is held tightly in a pair of pliers and forced into the hole in the chassis. The kink in the center holds the line cord securely, and the outside notches snap behind the lip of the hole to keep the entire assembly in place. Always put a strain relief on an appliance if it has none, and be sure it holds the wire firmly in order to keep any strain from being placed on the electrical connections.

If the body of the appliance normally gets very hot (such as a waffle iron), don't use soft rubber grommets or anything that would be damaged by heat. Instead, use the hard fiber grommets made especially for the purpose.

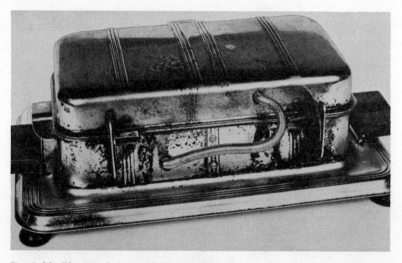

Fig. 1-20. The spiral device shown between the two halves of this waffle iron isn't a spring, but a flexible steel protector surrounding the interconnecting leads. The leads themselves are made of stranded copper to hold up under the constant flexing and heat, and are heavily wrapped with asbestos.

Two appliances whose line cords require special protection, because of the high heat and frequent movement to which they are subjected, are irons and waffle irons. An iron, of course, needs more attention, since its cord is constantly being pulled, twisted, and bent during use. This was one of the big reasons why the detachable plug was eliminated in favor of a permanently attached cord.

Fig. 1-19 shows a typical cord for an iron. The tapered rubber sleeve on the end keeps the wire from being bent too sharply and eases the strain from continual pulling and twisting. When repairing iron cords, be sure to replace this sleeve if it is missing or worn.

Waffle irons and similar appliances have two heating elements, one on the lid and one on the bottom. The interconnecting wires are wrapped tightly in asbestos and enclosed in a spiral springlike protector, shown in Fig. 1-20 (rubber wouldn't do at all because of the excessive heat). Check the wiring inside these appliances every time they are serviced to make sure there are no worn places to cause a short circuit.

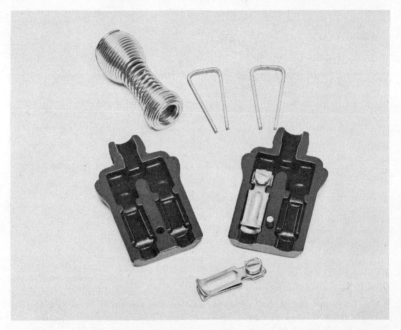

Fig. 1-21. An appliance plug disassembled. The channels or grooves inside the shell serve as strain reliefs to hold the wire tightly, should the user make a practice of disconnecting the plug by pulling it out by the cord. The actual contacts are also held in grooves. A spiral spring at the rear of the plug prevents the cord from being bent too sharply; the entire unit is held together by two small machine screws.

APPLIANCE CONNECTORS

Heavy-duty detachable appliance connectors, although no longer used on irons, are used extensively with waffle irons, grilles, toasters, coffee makers, and numerous other appliances.

These plugs are alike except in size. Fig. 1-21 shows one disassembled. The very heavy contacts allow the plug to carry up to a kilowatt without overheating, and the channels or grooves in the shell provide an automatic strain relief for the line cord. When reassembling these plugs, be sure to neatly dress the wire down in the grooves; otherwise the shell may be broken when the screws are tightened.

Fig. 1-22. Method of preparing an asbestos heater cord for installation. At the left, the wire is cut and ready for stripping. The asbestos is folded back and the insulation stripped from the ends of the wires (center). At the right, the asbestos fibers are held in place by wrapping thread around them, and circular lugs are attached to the ends of the wires.

Almost all connectors provide line-cord protection, such as the spring shown or a rubber sleeve. It should be in place before reassembling the plug. (Slip it over the wire *first*, and then put the plug together.)

There is a special way of preparing the cord for attachment to this type of plug. First, carefully slit the outer jacket about two inches from the end, and clip it off. Separate the wires and remove about ¾ inch of insulation from the ends (Fig.

1-22). Rewrap the asbestos around each wire, up to the exposed part. Now take a spool of common fine thread and wrap it tightly around each wire. The thread wrapping keeps the asbestos in place and thus makes the wire much easier to handle.

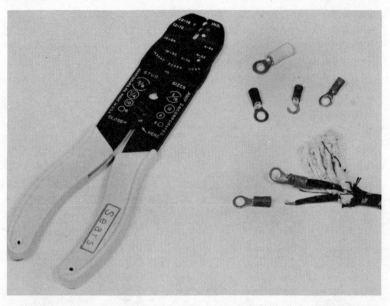

Fig. 1-23. Method of connecting special lugs for heavy-duty operation, such as irons and other devices using heating elements that require a large current. These lugs require no solder; the stripped wire is slipped into the lug and secured by the use of a crimping tool. The tool is applied twice—once where the bare wire touches the lug and once over the insulation. Different styles are available.

Attach lugs to the ends of the wires (Fig. 1-23) if the plug is big enough to hold them. If not, tin the ends well and loop each one to fit the connecting screw. Tighten these screws securely, for they will be carrying a heavy current; if loose, they will arc and develop a high resistance, in addition to overheating. (Motto in all work like this: a clean, tight connection is a cool one!)

If the cord is being attached to an iron, use connecting lugs like the type in Fig. 1-23. Notice that no solder is used in these lugs because the temperature of the connections is ordinarily above the melting point of solder. This type of lug should be

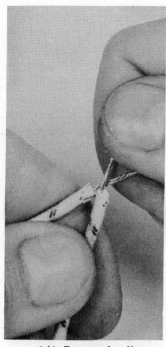

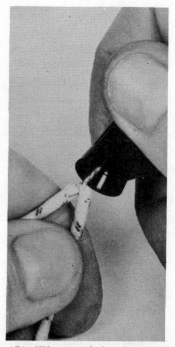

(A) Prepared splice.   (B) Wire nut being installed:

Fig. 1-24. Method of using a wire nut. The ends of the wires should be stripped back about ¾ inch. The wire nut should screw far enough onto the connection so that no bare wires will be left exposed.

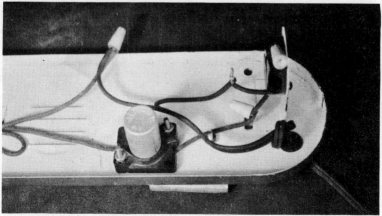

Fig. 1-25. Wire nuts such as these are often used to secure a splice. The two wires to be joined are twisted together as shown, and the wire nut is screwed over the connection, holding it securely.

crimped to both the wire and the insulation, and held tightly by the terminal nuts.

FASTENERS AND WIRE NUTS

The common terminal screw is used for almost all electrical connections in appliances. However, where it is necessary to fasten wires to wires without any terminals (a typical example is the motor leads of a mixer), a special fastener called a wire nut is used. This is made of cone-shaped plastic or ceramic, with a threaded hole in the center.

The method of using this device is illustrated in Fig. 1-24. The insulation is stripped from the ends of the wires to be joined, and the wires are twisted together as shown in Fig. 1-24A. The wire nut is then screwed tightly onto the connection until it covers the insulation (Fig. 1-24B). The ends of the wires should not be stripped back too far—about ¾ inch or so is usually enough. The wire nut should screw onto the connection far enough so that no bare wires will be left exposed when the connection is completed. (Some versions use a small conical brass spring instead of the molded threads.) Fig. 1-25 shows wire nuts used in a lighting fixture.

Chapter 2

Heating Elements

A lot of home appliances are basically nothing more than heating elements. Electric irons, toasters, coffee pots, space heaters, and hair dryers are some examples. Each has a power supply (the line cord) and a control (which can be a simple switch) or a thermostat (to regulate the amount of heat). The heating element itself is a special electrical conductor; when this is connected across the ac line, current flows through it. It has resistance, so it gets hot. These are made of special alloys so that they won't oxidize and burn up. You'll find heating elements made like coiled springs, flat ribbons, and straight wires wound in mica plates. The newest version is a quartz rod, which looks like glass but is a conductive compound. For special applications, the heating element is sealed in a metal tube or plate, with insulation to keep it from touching the metal. This type is used in coffee pots and similar applications where the heating element must be immersed in water.

Early electric hot plates used coiled-spring-type elements mounted in grooves in a ceramic material, as shown in Fig. 2-1. Later versions used sealed elements in disc-shaped cases, as shown in Fig. 2-2. Each element is rated in watts, meaning the amount of current it takes times the voltage. For a given resistance, the more current that flows, the higher the wattage. Since the voltage will be the same, we regulate the heat by making the elements of different resistances; the lower the resistance, the greater the current and the wattage.

CONTROLLING THE HEAT

We control the amount of heat in two ways. One is by use of a selector switch, which connects one, two, or three sections of the heating element into the circuit. For example, if we had a heater with three 100-watt elements, one element would give 100 watts of heat; to get 200 watts, we switch in one more, and so on. To obtain constant temperatures with a single element,

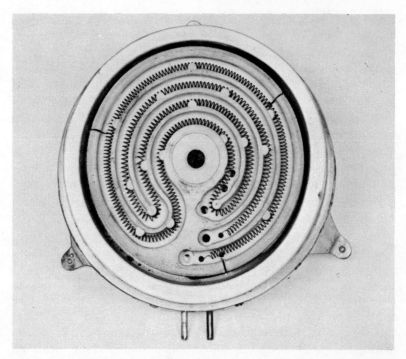

Fig. 2-1. An older-type "hot plate" with an exposed heating element mounted within the circular recess of a ceramic insulator (often referred to as a "brick").

we use a device called the *thermostat*—literally, *constant heat*. This is an automatic switch operated by heat, which automatically turns the power on and off in order to keep the temperature constant to within a few degrees.

The heart of all thermostats is a bimetal blade (Fig. 2-3), a strip of metal made from two unlike alloys—one with a high rate of expansion when heated and the other with a low rate. When heated (Fig. 2-3A), the high-expansion metal is *held* by the one with a low rate, and the combination of forces causes the blade to bend, as shown in Fig. 2-3B. When the heat is removed, the blade returns to its normally straight position.

This action can be used to control the heat from an electric heater. This is done by placing the bimetal blade where the heat from the main heating element will raise its temperature. When the heat rises above a predetermined level (fixed by the design of the thermostat blade), the blade bends, opening the contact; and the heating element cools off. When the temperature of the blade (and apparatus) drops to a lower limit, the blade straightens out once more, closing the contact; and the heating element goes on again. This process is repeated constantly while the appliance is on.

By altering the proportion and alloy of the two metals in the blade, thermostats can be designed to give almost any desired temperature control. All thermostats have an upper limit (the temperature at which the contacts open) and a lower limit (the temperature at which they close). In precision applications they can be made so sensitive that the temperature is kept constant to within one degree. Ordinary appliance thermostats do not have to be quite so sensitive.

The thermostats in the more common appliances are almost always adjustable. Fig. 2-4 shows some thermostats used in electric irons. The temperature of the iron is controlled by a screw, which varies the distance between the contact points and thus the amount the temperature must rise to open them. After this temperature is reached, the thermostat keeps the iron at the desired heat (within 5 to 7 degrees). Similar applications are found in all coffee makers, toasters, electric blankets, and other heat-producing appliances. Sometimes the temperature-controlling action of the thermostat is combined to provide a timing action. For instance, in some toasters a small heating element is wound around the thermostat blade. The current drawn by the main heating element flows through this smaller element and heats the blade. The auxiliary element is of such a size that it causes the blade to warp and open the contacts within a preset time. This device is used to make toast just the right shade or to boil coffee for so many minutes, and in many other applications requiring timed heat.

Fig. 2-2. A "hot plate" employing sealed elements. The elements themselves are enclosed in a solid ceramic brick which is sealed into a metal housing. The unit at the bottom center is a switch that permits selection of various degrees of heat.

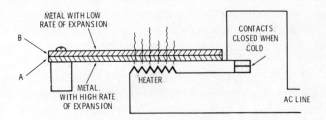

(A) *Blade cool, beginning to heat up.*

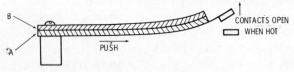

(B) *Blade hot.*

Fig. 2-3. Thermostatic action of a bimetal blade. Metal "A" has a high rate of expansion with heat, and metal "B" a low expansion rate.

TESTING AND REPAIRING HEATING ELEMENTS

Heating elements are easy to test. If they don't heat up, there is one of two possible causes. One, the element itself is open, or two, there is no power getting to it. The second can be checked with the little test lamps. If the power is on and the lamp glows when connected to the ends of the element, then the element is almost certainly open. To verify this, disconnect the power and read its resistance with the ohmmeter. If this shows an open circuit, you're sure. Be sure to check the connections on the terminals of the element. Due to the high temperature at which they operate, they can develop a bad elec-

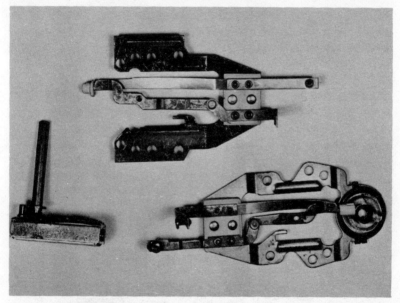

Fig. 2-4. Typical thermostats used with electric irons. Although they come in many sizes and shapes, their function remains the same—to control the amount of heat.

trical contact. Arcing at the terminals of an element when the power is turned on is a sure sign of a bad contact. Take the connection apart and clean it thoroughly. Put it back together and make sure that the wires, lugs, etc., are very tight. A loose connection will arc and cause trouble.

In some of the coiled-type elements discussed later, a break in the element is obvious. If the break is near the end, you can clean the wire and stretch it to reach the terminal again. This will be all right; it will make the element get just a little hotter, since you've reduced the resistance just a little. Don't take out more than 2 to 3 inches of such an element.

If these elements break near the middle, you can't solder them together; this type of wire will not take solder. Also, the element runs well above the melting point of ordinary solder. Special splicing *sleeves* can be used; the ends of the wire are slipped through the sleeve, and it's crimped (carefully!) with the tool shown in Fig. 1-7 or a pair of diagonal cutters. Most of the time it's better to replace a broken element, since it's probably ready to break in another place.

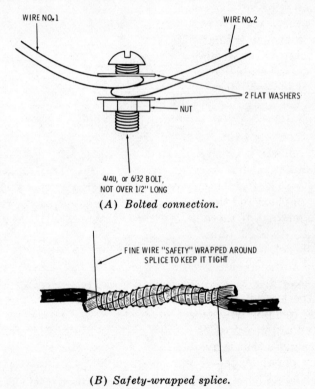

WIRE NO. 1

WIRE NO. 2

2 FLAT WASHERS

NUT

4/40, or 6/32 BOLT,
NOT OVER 1/2" LONG

(A) *Bolted connection.*

FINE WIRE "SAFETY" WRAPPED AROUND
SPLICE TO KEEP IT TIGHT

(B) *Safety-wrapped splice.*

Fig. 2-5. Two methods of splicing a wire carrying heavy current.

Sealed elements can't be repaired. In practically all cases, the replacements will have to be exact duplicates of the originals since they fit into tight spaces, etc. The coiled elements can be replaced with *universal* types. These are available at electrical supply stores, hardware stores, and others.

When replacing any heating element, be sure to get one with exactly the same wattage as the original (check the label on the appliance). This label will be on the case, usually near the point where the line cord goes into it. Sometimes the wattage will be stamped into the metal case.

In a few cases, you'll find connecting wires broken. It's better to replace these with a length of new wire. However, if you must make a splice, remember that the splice must be able to carry heavy currents. Many units use heavy braided wire, known as "copper rope," to handle the current without loss. In some applications, small ceramic beads are used as insulation; others use a wrapping of asbestos. Be sure to replace worn or broken insulation to prevent a shock or fire hazard.

Splicing wires in high-current circuits can be difficult. The joint must be able to carry the same current as the original wire; if loose or dirty, it will immediately overheat and burn out. It isn't possible to solder the joints in these wires, especially on large heating elements, because the wiring often runs above the melting point of ordinary solder. So, unless you use silver solder, the best way is to wrap the ends of the wire around a small bolt and nut placed between two flat washers (Fig. 2-5A), tightening the whole thing to hold the wires firmly in place and thus keep the joint resistance low. An alternative method, if there is enough original lead left, is to make a tightly twisted joint, winding at least three turns of wire around each other. This can be "safetied" by wrapping it with several turns of fine wire pulled very tight (Fig. 2-5B). Always clean the ends of the wires thoroughly so the joint will have the lowest possible resistance. If there is enough room, a small ceramic wire nut can be used.

When a splice must be insulated, there is a special tape made of fiber glass that is available for this purpose. Never use friction or plastic tape—it wouldn't last five minutes under the terrific heat! If no fiber glass tape is on hand, discarded asbestos insulation from a wire can be used. Wrap it tightly around the joint and tie it in place with long fibers of asbestos.

Chapter 3

Portable Table Ovens

One electrical appliance has become very popular over the past few years. This one is about as simple as you can get—just a metal box with a heating element in it. You'll find it called a rotisserie, broiler, warmer, sandwich grille and so on, but the most common name seems to be "table oven." You can make toast, warm up sandwiches, or even thaw frozen foods in it right at the table. We'll start with the simplest type and work our way up to the more elaborate units.

This table oven has a flat metal case, usually provided with a slide-in tray. The heating element is mounted on ceramic insulators located in the top of the case. Fig. 3-1 shows the heating element and an inside view of the cabinet. Some of the more elaborate types have insulated cabinets, and even the smallest have dual thicknesses of metal on all sides. The most common heating element is the spiral-wire type shown here; some of the units use the same sealed-unit type of heating elements used in electric ranges. The spiral-wire type uses Nichrome wire stretched over ceramic supports. The supports slip into notches stamped out of the inner liner, and the tension of the spring element holds them in place.

The heating element is attached to a two-prong plug on the cabinet. The two prongs of the connector are mounted on a small tab stamped out of the cabinet. This one uses a pair of ceramic blocks as insulators, one on either side of the metal. The holes in the metal are made large enough to let shoulders on the insulators fit snugly inside. This keeps the metal prongs from touching the metal of the case, which would cause a short or a dangerous shock hazard. A shoulder on the prongs fits against the outside of the insulator, and the inner end is threaded. Nuts and washers are used to hold the resistance wire. The wire is twisted around the "screw," and a metal washer is used to keep it in place and to keep the nut tightened. The rest of the wire is cut off or twisted around the element to keep it from shorting to the other elements. The inside of these units uses a highly polished metal surface to reflect the **heat onto the food being cooked.**

Fig. 3-1. Inside view of a typical portable table oven, showing the spiral-wire heating elements. The element is a spiral Nichrome wire stretched over ceramic supports. It is attached to a two-prong plug that is mounted on a small tab stamped out of the cabinet.

Fig. 3-2 shows an exterior view of the connector prongs and another way of mounting them on the metal case. Here, the prongs are insulated by thick mica washers on each side. The inner ones have shoulders which fit inside the hole to keep the prongs centered. Flat washers are used on the outside, with flat metal washers on each side so that the fragile mica will not be damaged by tightening the mounting nuts. As you can see, the base of each prong is made in the shape of a nut with hexagonal stamping, so that a nutdriver type of wrench can be used to hold the outer end while the nuts are tightened on the inside. Two nuts are used on each: the inner nut holds the prong tightly to the case, and the outer one holds the heating-element wires to the prong for electrical contact.

Fig. 3-2. An exterior view of the connector prongs and another way of mounting them on the metal case. The prongs are insulated by thick mica washers on each side. The inner washers have shoulders which fit inside the hole to keep the prongs centered.

These prongs *must* be very tight so that they cannot slip to one side and short to the metal case. If they loosen, retighten them, making sure that all of the insulating washers or ceramic insulators are set in the holes properly. If the mica washers are cracked or broken or if the ceramic insulators are broken, put new ones on in their place. Do not take any chances of causing a short to the case. After making repairs to these plugs, test for shorts between the case and the ac line, with the test lamp or neon tester. You can do this by connecting one side of the test lamp to a grounded object such as a water pipe, plugging the oven in, and touching the case with the other terminal of the test lamp. *Do not* touch the metal with your bare hand until you have made this test.

Many table ovens are equipped with thermostats to control the heat. Such a unit is shown in Fig. 3-3. A metal plate covers the odd-shaped hole in the case. A plastic knob on the thermostat shaft in the center is used to set it to the desired temperature. One lead from the plug goes directly to the heating element. The other, using heavy, asbestos-insulated wire, goes through the thermostat unit. These thermostats are replaceable and work exactly as the others discussed earlier on other heating-type appliances. Fig. 3-4 shows how to remove the control knob on this type of unit. A small setscrew must be

Fig. 3-3. Thermostat control used on table ovens. One lead from the plug goes directly to the heating element. The other is a heavy asbestos-insulated wire and goes through the thermostat unit.

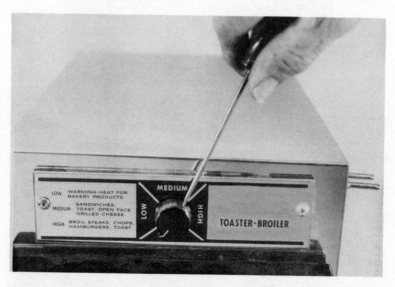

Fig. 3-4. Control panel on a typical table oven. The knob can be removed by loosening the small setscrew. When putting the knob on, turn the thermostat shaft all the way counterclockwise and put the knob on the shaft so the indicating mark lines up with the low mark on the plate and tighten the setscrew.

loosened, and the knob then comes off the shaft. If the knob works loose by itself, as they often do, the calibration of the thermostat will be wrong. To reset it, turn the thermostat shaft all the way counterclockwise, put the knob back on so that the arrow or indicating mark is lined up with the *low* mark on the plate, and tighten the screw again. This will work in the opposite direction, of course, if you turn the shaft all the way clockwise and set the pointer at the *high* mark. Two small Phillips-head screws hold the cover plate on the case. Some of these units are pretty elaborate; they have push-

Fig. 3-5. Front view of a typical rotisserie. Push-button switches on the front panel allow the unit to be used as a rotisserie, broiler, or toaster. A small electric motor turns the spit which is provided for roasting fowl and meat.

button control units, built-in timers, and many other convenient features. However, they are all basically the same—a heating element plus whatever controls are used.

ROTISSERIES

A mechanized version of this type of appliance is shown in Fig. 3-5. The heating elements, etc., are generally the same, but a rotating spit is provided for roasting fowl and meat. A small electric motor is mounted in one end of the case to turn the spit. Push-button switches on the front panel allow the unit to be used as a rotisserie, broiler, or toaster. A thermostat holds the heat at whatever level is desired, and a built-in timer unit will make the unit run for any desired length of time and then turn itself off.

Timer

Some rotisseries are equipped with a timer to permit cooking for a predetermined length of time. Fig. 3-6 shows a rotisserie using such a timer. The side cover of the unit has been removed to illustrate the positions of the various components. Inside the end cover you can see the heat-control switch at the

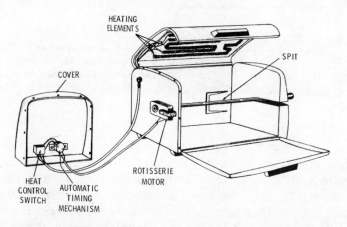

Fig. 3-6. Some rotisseries are equipped with a timer to permit cooking for a predetermined length of time. The side cover of this unit has been removed to illustrate the positions of the various components.

left; the automatic timing mechanism is located to the right. Both are set by the control knobs located on the outside cover. The heating element is mounted underneath the lid as shown and may be either an exposed or a sealed unit. A small motor, mounted on the side, drives the spit.

Heating Element

Replacement heating elements for the spiral-wire type can be found at any hardware store, appliance dealer, or electrical-parts supply store. Fig. 3-7 shows a typical replacement element on a card. This one is a 600-watt unit, as you can see from the label. Be sure to check the *rating plate* on your appliance; the correct wattage will be stamped on this plate or stamped into the metal case of the unit. Some are 600 watts, and others will be 1000-watt types. In the units which use sealed heating elements, you will have to get an *exact-duplicate* type from the dealer for that brand of appliance, so that it will fit into the insulators properly.

We might get in some facts about electrical heating elements like this that are often confusing to those who have never heard the correct explanation. If we have a 600-watt heating element and we need a 300-watt one, we *do not* cut the 600-watt

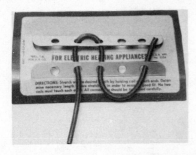

Fig. 3-7. A replacement heating element on a card. These come in different wattages so be sure to check the wattage rating of the appliance.

element in half. Instead, we *add* another 600-watt element in series with the first, so that the current has to flow through both. By hooking the two elements in series, we double the resistance so that only half as much current flows; therefore, we dissipate only half as much electrical *power*. If you want to go deeper into this fascinating subject, obtain any good textbook on basic electricity and look up *Ohm's law*.

When you replace one of the spiral-wire elements, make sure that you get a good *clean* connection to the terminal prongs. If the inner ends of the prongs are rusted or burned, replace the prongs while you are at it. If you fail to do this, you will have a loose connection on the inside ends, and there will be arcing. This will burn up the terminals in short order, and you will have the job to do over again. If an element like this has broken very close to one end, you can clean the wire, take the broken end off the terminal, and fasten the unbroken section back. Make a small loop in the end of the wire so that it will make good contact with the end of the prong. You can get enough slack to make the wire reach the terminal by stretching the remaining wire a little. In an element of this kind with a total "stretched length" of approximately 20 inches, you can break off 3 or 4 inches and make a new connection without causing too much trouble. The element will run hotter because the remaining wire has less electrical resistance. If too much of the resistance wire is taken off, it will run so hot that it will probably burn out again in a short time.

Now let's replace a spiral element. Start by making a good connection at one end. You can follow the path of the original element over the insulators by looking for the notches in their sides; the element goes into these to keep it in place. Follow the original path around the insulators until you get back to the other side of the plug. These insulators are held in place by the spring tension of the spiral element. Make sure that they are firmly in place in the notches, so that they will not come loose and let the element fall off. The elements look like springs, and they are springs, to a certain extent. However, they will not spring back as a true spring does; once stretched too far, they will "take a set" and stay stretched. Since we *need* this tension to hold the element firmly in place, be careful. It is a good idea to follow the original path with the new element, see how it goes, and then leave only one insulator out of it, temporarily. Then fasten the loose end to the plug, and very carefully stretch the new element over that last insulator and let it snap back into place. If the element is accidentally stretched too far so that it hangs loosely on the insulators, you can tie it to a couple of the insulators by wrapping one or two turns of bare wire around the element and the insulator. Twist the ends and clip them off closely. *Never* let the element or any tie wires rest so that they could touch the metal of the case.

Keep the prongs of the plug bright and clean at all times. In all heavy-current appliances, plugs and sockets tend to get dirty and corroded from arcing. Once they do get dirty, they get very hot and arc even more. This makes them get hotter and arc still more, and so on; the final result is the replacement of the plug and socket. The plug on the cord can be taken apart and cleaned if there seems to be any trouble. Keep the connections tight. You can check them by pushing the plug onto the prongs and pulling it off again. You ought to feel a very definite *resistance* when you do this, indicating that the plug is making a good tight connection. If the plug slips on the prongs very easily, it is too loose. Tighten it up until you have to push pretty hard to get it seated. One way of avoiding unnecessary arcing when plugging or unplugging these appliances is to make sure that the current is turned *off* when the plug is put on or taken off. Plugging them in with the switch on will cause a heavy arcing, even at the line plug of the wall outlet. To turn them on and off, use the regular switch on the appliance; this is rated to carry the heavy current without excessive arcing.

Thermostats and Switches

The contacts on thermostats and built-in switches should be kept clean. If you hear arcing (a *frying* or raspy sound when the switch is closed), check the switch; it will probably be loose or burned enough to make poor contact. In some cases, the switch can be cleaned and tightened by bending the switch-arms slightly. If the contacts are badly burned, it is better to replace the switch.

Motors

The motors used on rotisseries are small synchronous types with reduction gears to give the unit less speed and more power. Fig. 3-8 shows a typical unit. This happens to be a de-

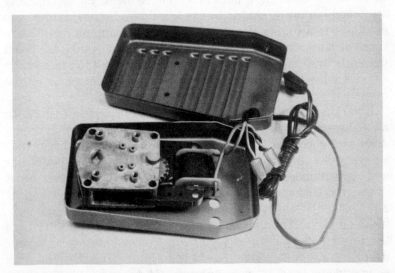

Fig. 3-8. Rotisserie drive motor with case opened. This motor housing hangs on the side of a barbecue cabinet. The motor is permanently mounted inside the cabinet on table models.

tachable type used with an outdoor grille or barbecue unit, but the motor and gearing are the same in most units. Note that there are no brushes; a solid rotor turns a small pinion gear, which drives a larger gear. This big gear drives another small pinion which turns the spit. The end result of this gear reduction is a speed of about 2 rpm.

Fig. 3-9. Showing the square hole in the rotisserie motor which is the drive chuck. The two bolt heads on each side of the chuck are used to hang this motor housing on the side of the barbecue cabinet.

The end of the spit fits into a square hole in the final gear shaft. This can be seen in the photo of Fig. 3-9. The two boltheads near the chuck are used to hang this motor housing on the side of the barbecue-unit cabinet. In the table models, the motor is permanently mounted inside the cabinet. Because of the slow speed and light loading, these motors do not give too much trouble. About the only electrical trouble you will find, aside from the customary open line cord, is an open coil in the motor. If it will not run at all, check for ac voltage across the coil, which is usually connected directly to the ac line. If there is voltage at this point, check the rotor by flipping it with a fingertip. If it is free to turn but refuses to even try to move when the power is turned on, then the coil is open. These coils can be replaced by taking out the bolts which hold the motor frame together. The laminated frame is built in two halves; the ends of one section meet inside the motor-coil core. The frame is taken apart, the old coil removed, and then the unit is reassembled with the new one. There is no polarity to this kind of coil; the motor will run the same way no matter which way the coil is put on the frame.

If the rotor tries to turn and the motor hums slightly, there may be some obstruction in the gears. Being used outdoors, there is always a chance that dust or dirt has accumulated until it is heavy enough to jam the gearing. With this type of motor, which has very low starting torque, no damage will occur. This type of motor will not chew up gears as a heavier motor will; it will simply stop. The gears can be cleaned by taking the motor unit out of the housing and washing them out with some kind of grease solvent, *not gasoline*. It will not hurt if some of this gets on the motor coil, but this usually is not necessary. Any dirt or dust can be washed out of the gear unit by immersing it in the solvent in a small can or dish and by loosening the dirt with an old paintbrush.

Relubricate with some kind of light grease, such as Lubriplate. Better still, use one of the new silicone greases, which will stay on the gears even at high temperatures. Oil will drip off and be pretty messy, even if it does not get into the food. Because of the low speed, the unit will not need much lubrication in any event. There is one very common cause of trouble in this kind of equipment, as well as in any other equipment used under these circumstances—insects. If the motor unit is stored in a garage for the winter, the chances are that the all-too-common wasp called the *mud dauber* will build a nest. This happy little bug carries clay and makes a good-sized nest. Once this clay has dried, it gets very hard and can jam any kind of light machinery. They love ready-made holes, such as the ventilation holes in the motor case. This can cause a lot of trouble, for the thing must be taken apart and cleaned out thoroughly. The best way to avoid this is to cover the unit completely. Store it in a tight box of some kind, or wrap it with plastic sheeting until there is no place left where the wasps can get inside. Anything with a hole bigger than ¼ inch in diameter is simply irresistible to them, so keep temptation out of their way by covering things tightly.

Chapter **4**

Electrical Cooking Appliances

One class of electrical cooking appliances shares several features. This class includes waffle irons (since these are made mostly of aluminum, the term iron is being used incorrectly, but old usage hangs on!), electric griddles, skillets, etc. All of these have electric heating elements controlled by thermostats, and all have a thick cast-aluminum plate for the cooking surface. This surface is smooth in skillets and griddles, and a crosshatch pattern in waffle irons.

SKILLETS

In many electric skillets, the heating element will be a sealed unit, cast as a part of the "pan" itself. Fig. 4-1 shows one of these. The skillet can be immersed in water for washing, since the element is watertight. The control thermostat is a plug-in unit (and this must not be immersed in water, of course!). Fig. 4-2 shows the thermostat with the cover taken off. The long sensing element rod goes inside the bottom of the skillet. It is made of aluminum or copper, or some metal which transmits heat readily. The thermostat contacts are in the center. A small neon pilot light shows when the contacts are closed and the element is heating.

The thermostat contacts are accessible for cleaning or adjustment. On the other side, a calibrated dial lets the user set the skillet for any frying temperature desired. Fig. 4-3 shows the heating element, which roughly follows the contour of the bottom of the skillet.

SERVICING

Most appliances in this class will have a metal cover on the bottom, held in place by screws. Removing these screws will give you access to the connections. In the sealed-in unit shown here, there's not much use for this! If the element is open, you'll have to replace the whole pan. The thermostat and line cord are about the only repairable parts. Fortunately, the

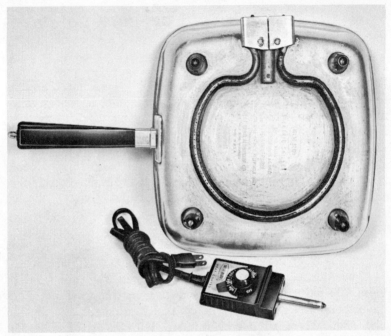

Fig. 4-1. Bottom view of an electric skillet. The heating element is in the aluminum casting, inside the ridge. The thermostatic control unit is in the large plug at the bottom.

sealed elements are very durable and give little trouble.

The thermostats can be checked for correct temperature setting by filling the pan with cooking oil, etc., turning the power on, and putting an oven thermometer in the liquid. The calibration of the dial need not be too accurate, but should be fairly

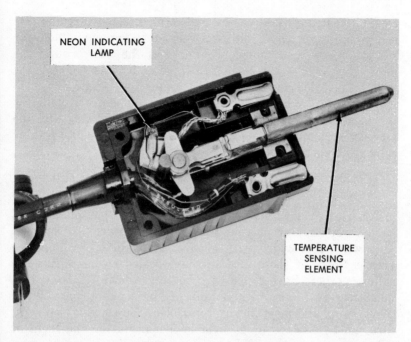

NEON INDICATING LAMP

TEMPERATURE SENSING ELEMENT

Fig. 4-2. A plug-in type thermostat control unit used with an electric skillet. This is the only repairable part on most skillets, since the heating element is sealed in. Some makes have this control built into the handle. Still, its function remains the same.

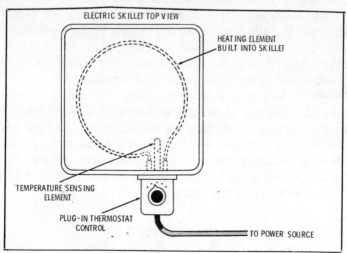

ELECTRIC SKILLET TOP VIEW

HEATING ELEMENT BUILT INTO SKILLET

TEMPERATURE SENSING ELEMENT

PLUG-IN THERMOSTAT CONTROL

TO POWER SOURCE

Fig. 4-3. The heating element and thermostat arrangement used on many electric skillets.

close to that indicated on the dial. Most thermostats like this can be adjusted; there will be a very small screw visible after the knob has been pulled off. Look all the way around the knob. If you see a very small screw, loosen it; this is a setscrew to hold the knob on tightly. If you can't see a screw, the knob will probably pull off. In some cases, you can "adjust" the thermostat by pulling the knob off, setting and checking the temperature, and putting the knob back on so that the pointer shows the correct temperature!

ELECTRIC GRIDDLES

The electric griddle, successor to the old "hot plate," will have a rectangular or round cast-aluminum cooking surface. This will be provided with grooves to drain off or hold the grease. Some of these griddles have sealed elements like the skillets; others have coiled-wire heating elements mounted on insulators just below the bottom of the cooking plate. Since they are all thermostatically controlled, the cooking temperature can be selected by a variable thermostat on the front of the case.

Let's clear up any possible confusion in a couple of terms commonly found in service literature on this subject. Any control which is *variable,* such as a thermostat, will have a shaft and knob and can be set with the fingers; no tools are needed. On the other hand, an *adjustable* control will have an adjusting screw, which must be set with a screwdriver or similar tool. There is no difference in the operation, only in the method of adjustment and/or calibration.

The griddles will usually be mounted in a small, flat case to protect the heating element and controls, and to keep heat away from whatever surface it's set on. Some will have covers for toasting sandwiches, etc.; others will be open-top types. To get to the heating element and controls, turn it over. If you see small screws at each corner of the bottom plate, take these out and remove the plate. All parts will be accessible.

WAFFLE IRONS

Waffle irons are constructed exactly like griddles. The "waffled" surface of the cooking plate will be mounted in a metal cabinet. In practically all of these, the heating element will be of the coiled type on insulators mounted on the case or sometimes on the bottom of the plate itself. Fig. 4-4 shows a waffle iron with a reversible plate so that the appliance can be used as a waffle iron or sandwich grille. Each plate is held in place by studs on one side that are slipped into slots in the case; the other side is held by a spring latch. This type is a "repairman's friend"! All you need do to make the heating element, thermostat, line cord, or anything else accessible is trip the latch and lift the plate.

A coiled element is used here. Notice the perforated metal shield over it. This is insulated from the element itself and protects the user should he or she decide to change sides on the plates while the unit is plugged in! Of course, you shouldn't do this, but if you do, you're safer!

The only difference between a waffle iron and the other types of appliances in this class is that here we have a top heat-

Fig. 4-4. A combination waffle iron and sandwich grill. The plates are reversible. One side is used for cooking waffles and the other side is used for grilling sandwiches.

ing element, so that both sides of the waffle will cook at the same time. Everything else is identical. The top part is on a special slotted hinge, so that the upper plate can rise with the waffle as it expands while cooking. The interconnecting leads between the bottom and top parts must be made of stranded wire, usually wrapped with flexible asbestos. These wires are normally enclosed in what looks like a very tightly coiled steel spring but is really a very flexible protector for the upper-plate wiring. You can see one of these in Fig. 1-20.

If the insulation on these leads should break, the leads will probably short and blow the fuse. If so, replace both leads with new wire and be sure to use a wire with many strands for the most flexibility. Never use anything but asbestos insulated wire here. The wires get pretty hot while the appliance is in use, and plastic or rubber insulation will melt.

WARMING PLATES

Warming plates are another type of electrical cooking appliance in the same category as waffle irons, griddles, and skillets. Basically, they are exactly like griddles but they don't get quite as hot. They're intended to keep food warm until served. Construction is about the same as an electric griddle—a flat metal surface which is heated by an element underneath. A low-wattage heating element is used. Servicing is the same as before. There will probably be a bottom plate to protect the heating element and controls. This plate is held in place by screws at the corners. Some have thermostats, others do not. If an element needs replacement, check the label to see what wattage you need.

Chapter 5

Electric Cookers and
Coffee Makers

Now, we get to another fairly large class of cooking appliances. These could be called "electric saucepans," and they were, at first. New models include a lot of specialized cookers under many different names. We could divide them into two major classes: *hot* and *warm.* In the hot class are such appliances as deep-fat fryers, popcorn poppers, rice cookers, and so on, which get pretty hot and, in general, stay that way. In the warm class, we find such things as bun warmers, fondue cookers, steamers, etc. These do not use high heat, but merely keep food warm until ready to serve. Of course, there are the usual combination appliances, which cook the food at a high heat, then automatically switch to a low heat to hold the food at serving temperature. You'll see this same idea used in quite a few other appliances on the following pages.

Appliances using constant heat, like the deep-fat fryer, use standard heating elements of the coiled or sealed types and variable thermostats. The desired temperature is set on the dial, and the unit will hold the heat at that level until turned off. Fig. 5-1 shows the spiral element used in one popcorn popper. No thermostat is used; you turn it off after all of the corn is popped. Popcorn poppers come in all sizes and shapes, but electrically they're all the same. Check the label to find the correct wattage for replacement elements. A standard appliance plug and line cord are used.

The *deep-fat fryer* is a constant-heat type, too. It consists of a deep metal pot, usually provided with a glass cover to contain spatters of grease if the food pops while cooking. This is a high-temperature device with an adjustable thermostat. Basically, it is the same as the electric skillet described in Chapter 4.

Heating elements can be spiral or sealed types. Many of these have a separate pot which can be taken off the heating element for washing. A few have the heating element sealed in the bottom of the unit; these can generally be immersed in water for washing. Check the instruction book or label to be sure. If the element is not sealed, you'll find the warning, "Do **not immerse in water.**"

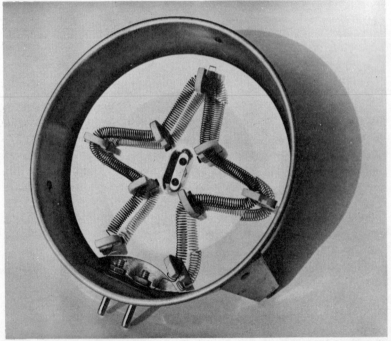

Courtesy Western Auto Co.

Fig. 5-1. The heating element used in one type of popcorn popper. This one is repairable. However, be sure to measure the length of the replacement wire accurately, in order to get the same operating temperature as before. Other types of poppers may use sealed elements. Again, it must be replaced by the exact duplicate, or the temperature will not be the same.

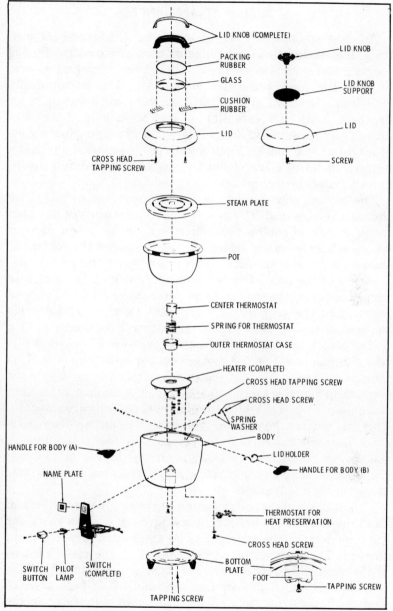

LID KNOB (COMPLETE)

PACKING RUBBER

GLASS

CUSHION RUBBER

LID

CROSS HEAD TAPPING SCREW

LID KNOB

LID KNOB SUPPORT

LID

SCREW

STEAM PLATE

POT

CENTER THERMOSTAT

SPRING FOR THERMOSTAT

OUTER THERMOSTAT CASE

HEATER (COMPLETE)

CROSS HEAD TAPPING SCREW

CROSS HEAD SCREW

SPRING WASHER

BODY

HANDLE FOR BODY (A)

LID HOLDER

HANDLE FOR BODY (B)

NAME PLATE

THERMOSTAT FOR HEAT PRESERVATION

CROSS HEAD SCREW

SWITCH BUTTON   PILOT LAMP   SWITCH (COMPLETE)

BOTTOM PLATE

FOOT

TAPPING SCREW

TAPPING SCREW

Courtesy Matsushita Electric Corp. of America

Fig. 5-2. An exploded view of a typical rice cooker. The cooking pot is separate, and the lid is perforated to allow steam to escape. The heating element and thermostats are located in the base.

DUAL-HEAT APPLIANCES

Another specialized class of appliance uses dual-heat controls. This includes electric coffee makers, rice cookers, fondue cookers, and several other types. These use a high heat at first to cook the food, brew the coffee, etc., then automatically switch to a low heat to keep the food warm until served. A lot of these, with the exception of coffee makers, have separate pots for easier washing. Fig. 5-2 shows an exploded view of a typical rice cooker. The cooking pot is separate and has a perforated lid to allow steam to escape. The heating element and thermostats are in the base.

The heating element here is a dual-heat sealed unit. Two thermostats are used. The first is a special center type mounted in the middle of the heating element. It has a sort of *plunger* on top which is spring loaded so that it touches the bottom of the cooking pot at all times. This lets it sense the actual temperature of the pot. After keeping the heat high for a certain period of time, the center thermostat opens and the second thermostat, the *keep-warm* thermostat takes over and holds the cooked food at whatever temperature is desired.

The center thermostat is a special type used in several different appliances. Fig. 5-3 shows a cutaway drawing of it. This thermostat uses a piece of semiconductor material—a *ceramic magnet*. When the thermostat is cold, the magnet attracts a small piece of iron to which the electrical contacts are attached. This magnet has the peculiar property of losing its magnetism after it reaches a certain temperature! When this happens, the spring pulls the iron away, opening the contacts. When the ceramic magnet cools off again, it regains its magnetic attraction and is ready to go.

This property is used for timing purposes. When the bottom of the pot reaches a certain temperature and stays there for the time desired, the magnet lets go and switches off the main element. The time setting is determined by the material used in the magnet and its design. This type is not adjustable. The units are all sealed and are not repairable. If it fails to make contact, it must be replaced with an exact duplicate, or the appliance will not work properly any more.

The *warm* thermostat in this unit is a standard bimetal-blade type. It is set to open at a low temperature. You can see

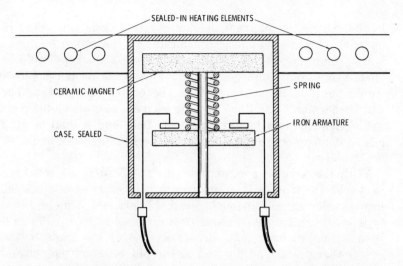

Fig. 5-3. A cutaway drawing of a thermostat mounted in the middle of the heating element. When the thermostat is cold, the ceramic magnet at the top attracts a small piece of iron that the electrical contacts are attached to. After it reaches a certain temperature, the magnet loses its magnetism, allowing the spring to pull the iron away, which opens the contacts.

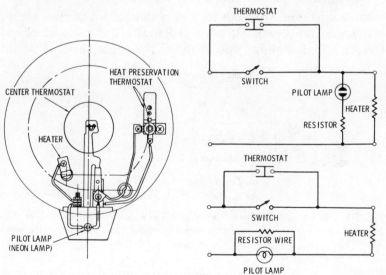

Courtesy Matsushita Electric Corp. of America

Fig. 5-4. Schematic diagram and wiring diagram of a dual-heat appliance. The warm thermostat, which is connected in parallel with the magnetic thermostat in the center, is a standard bimetal-blade type. This thermostat opens at a low temperature.

in the schematic diagram of Fig. 5-4 that it is connected in parallel with the magnetic thermostat in the center.

One common complaint with appliances of this type could be "gets warm, but won't get hot enough to cook properly." This would point to a bad contact on the center thermostat. The warm thermostat and the heating element are all right. This model has a single heating element. If it had a dual-heating element, an open circuit in one of the *hot* elements could be the problem.

With the reverse symptom where the food cooks but then gets cold, the trouble is in the keep-warm thermostat, since the heating element is obviously good. If this is a bimetal-blade type with accessible contacts, it can be cleaned up and adjusted. For an easy test, disconnect one of the leads to the center thermostat and try it. You can put water in the pot and check it with a thermometer to see if it is keeping the contents at the right temperature.

COFFEE MAKERS

Coffee makers, although they vary quite a bit in size, shape, and appearance, will all have practically the same electrical circuit. Fig. 5-5 shows one of these. Note that the thermostat

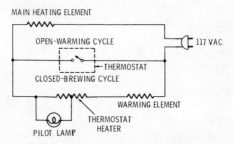

Fig. 5-5. *The wiring arrangement used on many automatic coffee makers. The brewing cycle occurs when the thermostat is closed; the warming cycle when its open.*

contacts are connected *across* the warming element and pilot light. When the unit is plugged in, these contacts are closed. The warming element is shunted (shorted out) so only the main heating element is in the circuit. This is the largest element. When the coffee maker has been on long enough to complete the brewing cycle, the thermostat contacts open. Now, the warming element, thermostat heater, and brewing element are all connected in *series*. This causes the voltage to divide up among all of them, and the current goes down. So, the heat developed is quite a lot less than if only the big brewing element is used. Notice that the pilot lamp is connected across a part of the thermostat heater. During the brew cycle, this whole circuit is shunted out. When the thermostat contacts open, current flows through the heater; the small voltage drop developed makes the pilot lamp light, indicating that the coffee is ready. These pilot lamps will ordinarily be low voltage radio types of 6 or 12 volts, etc.

Troubles in coffee makers will be the same as those in any other electric-heat devices—open heating elements, dirty thermostats, etc. Like all the rest, the line cord and plug will cause most of the troubles. Always make sure that they are in good shape before taking apart the coffee maker itself.

REPLACEMENT HEATING ELEMENTS

If the cord and thermostat are good, check the heating element. Disconnect both wires and check the element for continuity. If it reads open, it must be replaced. Due to the construction of most coffee makers, only an exact-duplicate heating element can be used. Fig. 5-6 shows some typical units. Those at the top are flat or plate types; others are cylindrical, etc. In older units, you can sometimes find "Universal" replacements, like the flat type. In later models, most of the elements will be of the sealed type, like that at the lower right, and fit only one make. You should order by brand name and model number.

Many units will use a sealed heating element, which has threads on one end of the case. These are held in place by a large, thin nut screwed onto these threads. Special seals, washers, and gaskets are used to prevent leakage. The exploded view of a modern coffee maker is seen in Fig. 5-7, showing how all of the various parts go together. Note the thermostat bracket, auxiliary heater, and other parts; these must all be reassembled in the correct order. Suggestion: if you do not have a service manual, WAIT until you get the new heating element before you take the old one out! When you do remove the old heating element, lay the various parts out on the bench in the order in which they came off. Then, put them back in the reverse order to avoid leaks, etc.

The easiest way to loosen the large nut holding the heating element is to use a large automotive-type socket wrench with an extension handle. In the case of the unit shown here, this would be a 1⅝-inch socket. The maker of this unit suggests clamping the socket wrench in the jaws of a vise, slipping the nut into it, then loosening the whole thing by turning the heating element itself with an adjustable wrench. This is shown in Fig. 5-8.

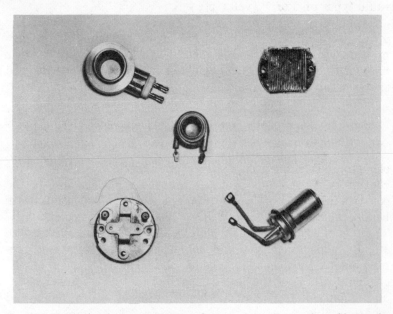

Fig. 5-6. Typical replacement heating elements for coffee makers. Notice the two types, cylindrical and flat. Some of these will fit quite a few different units; others are "special" and fit only those models for which they are designed.

Fig. 5-9 shows a bottom view of a coffee maker. A nut on the end of a long bolt holds the case of the heating element and the thermostat. Note the ceramic insulators coming through the bottom of the pot. Make sure that these are not cracked or broken; the wires from the new heating element must be passed through them for insulation. When replacing any

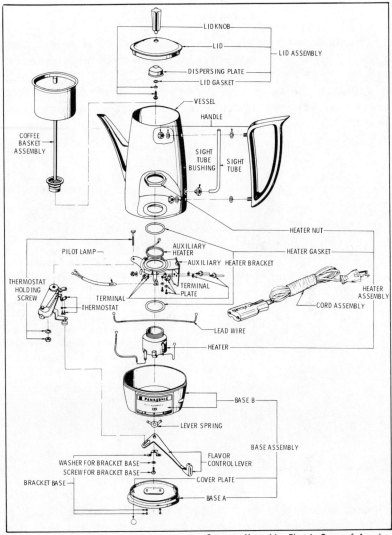

LID KNOB

LID

LID ASSEMBLY

DISPERSING PLATE

LID GASKET

VESSEL

HANDLE

COFFEE
BASKET
ASSEMBLY

SIGHT
TUBE
BUSHING

SIGHT
TUBE

HEATER NUT

PILOT LAMP

AUXILIARY
HEATER

HEATER GASKET

AUXILIARY HEATER BRACKET

THERMOSTAT
HOLDING
SCREW

TERMINAL
PLATE

HEATER
ASSEMBLY

TERMINAL

THERMOSTAT

CORD ASSEMBLY

LEAD WIRE

HEATER

BASE B

LEVER SPRING

BASE ASSEMBLY

WASHER FOR BRACKET BASE

SCREW FOR BRACKET BASE

FLAVOR
CONTROL LEVER

BRACKET BASE

COVER PLATE

BASE A

Courtesy Matsushita Electric Corp. of America

Fig. 5-7. An exploded view of a modern coffee maker. This shows all the various parts of the coffee maker and the correct order in which they must be reassembled.

sealed-case element like this, be sure that there are no dents, pieces of broken gaskets, etc., under the sealing lip of the case. Scrape everything very clean and replace any gaskets that have been damaged. Otherwise, you'll have leaks.

71

THERMOSTATS

Thermostats of all kinds and sizes are used. However, they all work in the same way. An exact replacement must be used if one cannot be cleaned up and repaired. Fig. 5-10 shows a pair of typical units. The one on the left has what is now a common feature—it can be adjusted to make the coffee stronger (brew longer) or weaker, as desired.

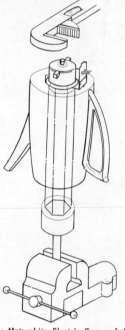

Fig. 5-8. To remove the heating element, use a large automotive-type socket wrench with an extension handle, a vise, and a large adjustable wrench. Place the socket wrench in the jaws of the vise and slip the nut into it; take the large adjustable wrench and turn the heating element.

Courtesy Matsushita Electric Corp. of America

General hint: Be careful when handling coffee makers. Most of them are made of highly polished aluminum. If one is rolled around on a dirty bench, it can be scratched and then you're in trouble! Always put the coffee maker on some kind of cloth pad. Minor scratches can be polished out, but it's easier to avoid them.

CALIBRATED THERMOSTATS

Many *adjustable* thermostats, like those on coffee makers, toasters, etc., are not accurately calibrated; they're simply marked "stronger-weaker," "lighter-darker," and so on. Many of the better cookers have thermostats with calibrated dials, so that the cooking temperature can be accurately adjusted. Such a unit is the Panasonic NF-851E Tempura-Fondue cooker seen in Fig. 5-11. The dial is calibrated from 180 to 400°F.

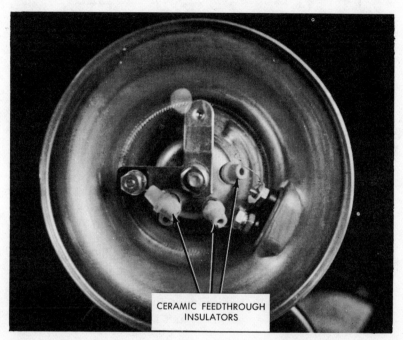

CERAMIC FEEDTHROUGH INSULATORS

Fig. 5-9. Bottom view of a coffee maker using a cylindrical heating element. The end of the long mounting bolt can be seen at the center. This bolt allows the element to be drawn down tightly against the bottom of the pot. The leads of the heating element are passed through holes which are insulated by ceramic beads.

These do not need frequent adjustment; however, if you want, you can check the dial for accuracy. Put oil in the cooker and set the dial to 280°F. Get a high-temperature thermometer (400°F or higher), and place it in the oil as shown in Fig. 5-11. Wait 20 minutes; the thermometer should read the same temperature for which the dial is set.

If it doesn't, the thermostat can be recalibrated with very little trouble. Pull off the thermostat knob and remove the thermostat knob plate. Push the thermostat knob back on, set

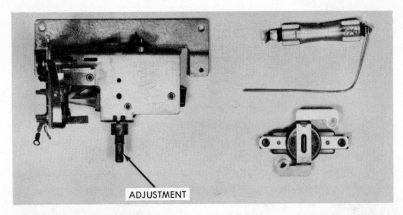

Fig. 5-10. *Typical replacement thermostats for automatic coffee makers. The unit at the right is not adjustable. The one at the left can be adjusted by moving the lever shown; this regulates the boiling time and hence the strength of the coffee.*

to 280°F. Check the thermometer reading (and be sure that *it* is accurate!). If the reading is low, say about 270°F, turn the small setscrew you can see inside the thermostat-knob shaft counterclockwise, just a little bit. Wait a few minutes and recheck the temperature of the oil. If the thermometer shows a higher temperature than the knob indicates, turn the setscrew clockwise. When you get through, lock the setscrew by putting a small dab of paint or nail polish on it. Replace the thermostat knob-plate and knob, and the job is done.

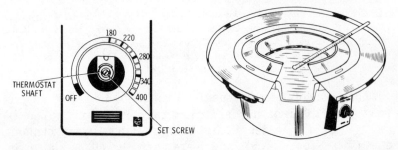

Fig. 5-11. *A fondue cooker. The thermostat on the left has a calibrated dial. To check the dial for accuracy, put oil in the cooker and set the dial to 280°F. Place a high-temperature thermometer (400°F or higher) in the oil and wait 20 minutes. If the temperature on the thermometer doesn't read the same as the dial, calibrate the thermostat.*

Chapter 6

Electric Irons

The *electric iron* is an appliance that has "always been with us"! It began as a simple gadget, consisting of the soleplate, handle, and a heating element. There were no controls; it got hot and stayed hot. Then, a thermostat was added to control the heat, and from there on things got complicated! The modern electric iron can steam, spray, squirt, and so on. The name doesn't fit it at all any more. There's very little iron; practically all of it is aluminum.

Fig. 6-1 shows an older type that has been disassembled. The heating element is under the sheet-metal cover, which is held to the soleplate by two screws. The handle at the top is held to the cover by hooks which slip into slots. The older types were often very difficult to get into; most of the fasteners were cleverly concealed and hard to get to. (Later models are much more accessible.) Elements were flat mica plates around which flat-wire heating elements were wound. The elements were insulated by sheets of mica. Fig. 6-2 shows two types. The flat ones at the top are fastened to the soleplate and connected by heavy asbestos-covered wires. At the bottom, the heating element is molded into the soleplate. The whole thing must be replaced if the element burns out.

The electrical circuit is the same as the heater-type appliances previously discussed: current flows through the line cord, through the thermostat, to the heating element, and that's all. Heating elements in earlier models were about 500-

to 700-watt types. In the modern models, heating elements up to 1200 watts are used. Sealed-element and flat-card types are used. This varies with the make and model. Exact-duplicate replacements are usually needed so that they will fit exactly into the space provided.

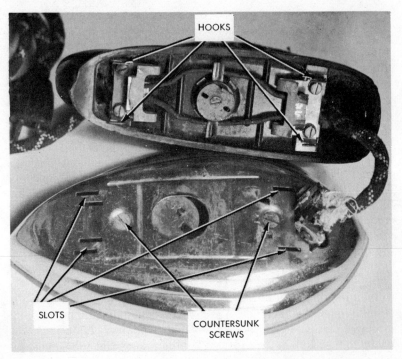

Fig. 6-1. An older-type dry iron partially disassembled. Dismantling an electric iron can be quite tricky unless you know the right "combination," as explained in the text.

STEAM IRONS

Electrically, there's no difference between steam irons and dry irons. A steam iron has a small reservoir mounted above the heating element. A control valve on this allows the water to drip slowly into recesses in the soleplate. A check valve keeps the water from going back up into the tank. When the water hits the hot element, it's converted to steam and goes out through holes in the bottom of the soleplate. Fig. 6-3 shows a diagram of the construction of a typical steam iron.

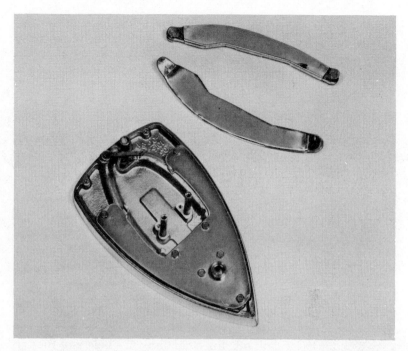

Fig. 6-2. Some typical replacement heating elements for electric irons. The flat ones at the top are fastened to the soleplate and connected by heavy asbestos-covered wires. The heating element is molded into the soleplate at the bottom.

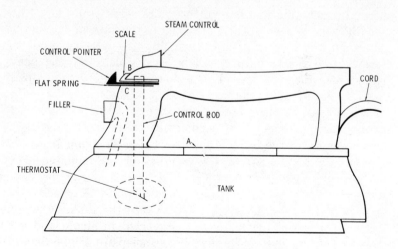

Fig. 6-3 Outline of a typical steam iron.

There are a few things here that are common to practically all steam irons. The control rod which goes down from the top of the handle to the thermostat itself is always mounted on the soleplate. This has a *yoke,* or slotted rod, which engages a mating slot in the thermostat. When you take the handle off, the rod lifts out. When you put the iron back together, be *sure* that this rod is correctly positioned in the thermostat, or it won't work. You can tell whether the rod is correctly positioned by turning the control pointer; if this moves freely, you missed the slot!

The water tank is filled through the filler tube. Here again, be sure that the pipe from this is properly placed in the hole in the tank. Check the steam-vent holes in the soleplate. Some water has minerals in it. In the course of time, the mineral residue will make a hard whitish deposit in the holes and clog them up. If the clogging isn't too bad, the deposit can be removed with some of the chemical cleaners. This is poured into the tank and allowed to set. Some types must be used when the iron is hot. Follow the directions on the chemical cleaner. If this doesn't free the holes, you can often open them manually with a small twist drill bit. Push this into the hole and turn it. Choose one that just fits the holes.

Fig. 6-4 shows a typical steam iron that has been disassembled. The thermostat control rod and filler tube can be seen on the front. In the older models, a heavy appliance plug was used; in fact, this was known for years as an *iron plug.* Now, the line cord is permanently attached to the back of the handle. There will be a small plastic cover plate over it. Take out the screws, and the terminals will be accessible. Note the heavy rubber sleeve on the cord. This is a strain relief which helps to keep the cord from breaking as a result of the constant bending of the cord as the iron is used. Be sure that this is firmly held in the clamp provided. The cord comes out of the handle at the side away from the user. Many irons provide a notch in both sides of the handle so that the cord can be installed for either a right- or left-handed user.

STEAM/SPRAY IRONS

Here again, the iron is the same. Now a tiny pump has been added so that hot water may be sprayed onto the cloth being

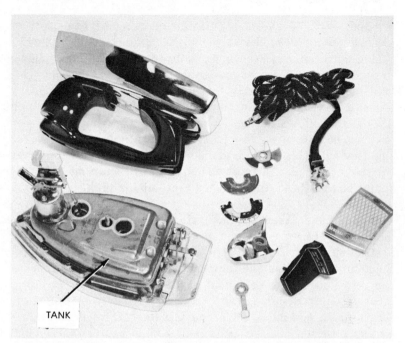

TANK

Fig. 6-4. A steam and dry iron disassembled. Notice the water tank located beneath the cover.

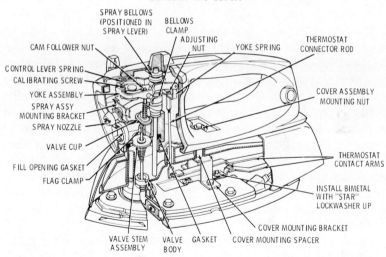

SPRAY BELLOWS
(POSITIONED IN
SPRAY LEVER)

BELLOWS
CLAMP

ADJUSTING
NUT

CAM FOLLOWER NUT

YOKE SPRING

THERMOSTAT
CONNECTOR ROD

CONTROL LEVER SPRING
CALIBRATING SCREW

YOKE ASSEMBLY

SPRAY ASSY
MOUNTING BRACKET

COVER ASSEMBLY
MOUNTING NUT

SPRAY NOZZLE

VALVE CUP

FILL OPENING GASKET

FLAG CLAMP

THERMOSTAT
CONTACT ARMS

INSTALL BIMETAL
WITH "STAR"
LOCKWASHER UP

COVER MOUNTING BRACKET

VALVE STEM
ASSEMBLY

VALVE
BODY

GASKET

COVER MOUNTING SPACER

Courtesy Westinghouse Electric Corp.

Fig. 6-5. A cutaway drawing of a steam/spray iron. The design of the handle of this iron permits easy conversion of the appliance from a right-hand iron to a left-hand iron.

pressed. Fig. 6-5 shows a cutaway drawing of one of these irons, showing all of the valves, pipes, and other "machinery."

One good point is seen here. Note the *mounting nut* shown in the recess in the cover, under the center of the handle. This holds the handle assembly to the body of the iron. In many types, after this one nut has been taken off, the handle will lift up and off, exposing the mechanism. In some irons, you may not be able to *see* this mounting nut at all. If not, look for small metal plates with no visible fastenings; these often cover the mounting nut; in most cases, they will snap off. Fig. 6-4 shows one of these, the polished plate at the right side of the photo.

If you have taken the mounting nut or bolt out and the handle still refuses to come free, don't use force! Something is still holding it. Shake it gently to see where it's still attached. Look for things like the temperature scale on the thermostat control; sometimes these hold parts of the unit in place and must be slipped out toward the front. Also, look for more screws, etc., concealed under nameplates (a favorite place!) and such things.

REPAIRS

Most iron repairs will be absurdly simple, electrically. An open element or a defective thermostat is about all that can happen. Broken line cords probably cause more trouble than all the rest put together. If the iron doesn't heat, take off the little plate covering the iron end of the line cord and check the cord for continuity. Most breaks happen at this end. Either a new cord can be put on, or about 6 inches of the old one can be cut off and the terminals replaced. When making connections at the iron, be sure that the terminals, lugs, and screws are very clean and tightly fastened. Due to the high currents drawn by the heating element, any dirt in the connections will make this joint overheat, causing even heavy terminal lugs to burn up due to the arcing.

Spray pumps, etc., can be repaired without too much trouble. Most of them are easy to take apart. Rods and shafts, etc., will be held together by small screws and clamps or by *C-rings* which can be pulled off with a pair of long-nose pliers. Most of the trouble in these parts is due to clogging of valves and nozzles by deposits of chemicals (mostly calcium). These can be cleaned out by carefully inserting small things (such as the drill bits mentioned before, needles, and so on) into the holes and turning them.

The soleplate of an iron will often pick up a coating of starch, etc., which makes the iron drag. This can be cleaned off by carefully polishing it with household cleaner. In stubborn cases, try some mild abrasive such as *rubbing compound* used for automobile finishes. Don't use sandpaper or anything like that, because it will scratch the soft aluminum of the soleplate and make it very hard to smooth out.

Chapter 7

Electric Toasters

The electric toaster could be the oldest electrical household appliance. It's been around for a long time. Fig. 7-1 shows what could have been *Model 1,* strictly a manual type. One heating element was used, and two slices of bread were held near this by the hinged lids. The lids were held up by springs. When one side of the bread was suitably charred, the lids were lowered; this flipped the bread over and toasted the other side. This type didn't even have a switch; when it was plugged in, it was on.

The next version was the two-slice type with three heating elements. The bread was placed on a rack and lowered between the heaters by pushing a lever. Both sides toasted at the same time. The first version of this was manual; then, this too was automated by the addition of a thermostat. The final improvement was to make the thermostat control the mechanical action of the bread racks. And lo, we had the *pop-up* toaster. Fig. 7-2 shows the basic construction. When the bread was toasted to the desired shade, the thermostat latch let go, and a spring raised the rack, turning off the heaters at the same time. Small metal guide rods kept the bread from touching the heating elements.

You'll find all sorts of apparent variations in modern toasters, but all are basically the same since they do the same things. Quite a few different versions of the mechanism for

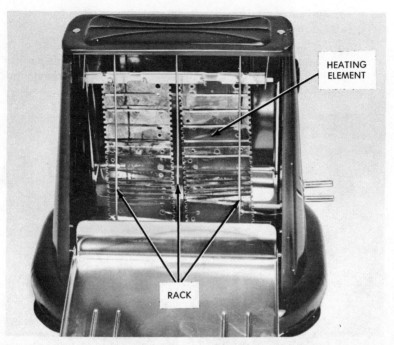

Fig. 7-1. Here is the simplest form of electric toaster—the manual type. The lids in each side lower as shown; the bread is placed against the rack, and the lids then released. Actually this unit consists of nothing but a heating element and a line cord.

Fig. 7-2. Basic construction of a pop-up toaster. This is a two-slice type with three heating elements.

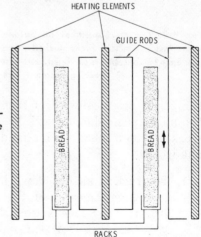

lowering and raising the bread make some types of toasters more fully automated, but each one is the same still.

Fig. 7-3 shows the latch and thermostat mechanism of a typical automatic pop-up toaster. The basis of this pop-up action is the timing. Sometimes this is done by the thermostat itself, sometimes by a small clockwork-type device or other

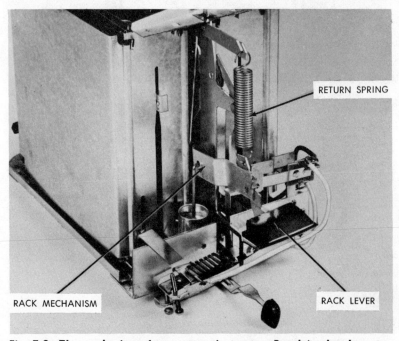

Fig. 7-3. The mechanism of an automatic toaster. Bread is placed on two racks inside, and the racks pushed down by the lever at the lower right. This not only latches the rack down, but also closes the switch that energizes the heating element and starts the timer.

things. In practically all of them, you will be able to see how the mechanism should work by taking the outer case off and working the mechanism by hand a few times. Here's how this one works:

1. The rack is pushed down by hand. This causes the latch to engage the catch on the frame and hold it down (Fig. 7-4A). The same action closes the main and auxiliary switches (Fig. 7-4B). Current flows through the heating elements and through the heater wrapped around the bi-

metal blade of the thermostat. When cold, this blade is straight. The toasting starts since the main heating elements are energized.

2. As the thermostat blade warms up, it starts to warp and bow up in the center (Fig. 7-4C). When this blade reaches maximum warp, the hook arm on the right side of the rack catches under the thermostat blade, holding it up. An extension of the hook arm (not shown) closes an auxiliary switch; this bypasses the *thermostat* heater, leaving only the main heating elements turned on.

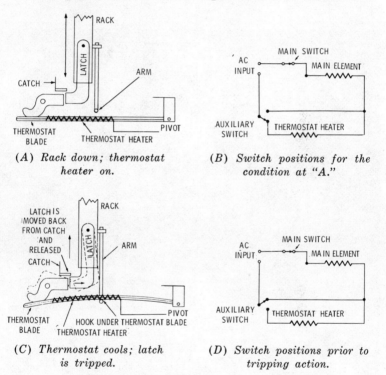

(A) *Rack down; thermostat heater on.*

(B) *Switch positions for the condition at "A."*

(C) *Thermostat cools; latch is tripped.*

(D) *Switch positions prior to tripping action.*

Fig. 7-4. An electromechanical timing control.

3. Without current flowing through the heater, the thermostat blade cools off. As it does so, it tries to straighten out. Since the center is being held up by the hook arm, its left end rises, causing the trigger arm to push the latch away from the catch. This lets the rack rise. As it does, the main switch opens, and the heating elements

cool off. Fig. 7-4D shows the circuit and the switch connections just prior to trip time.

Fig. 7-5 shows the thermostat from below; the toaster is standing on one end. Fig. 7-6 shows a close-up of the thermostat blade; you can see the hook arm, the rack lever, and the heater wound around the thermostat blade. The lever at the bottom is the *shade* adjustment; this can be set to make the toast lighter or darker by controlling the length of time needed to make the mechanism trip.

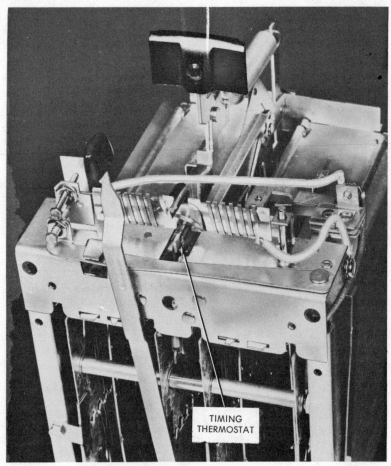

TIMING
THERMOSTAT

Fig. 7-5. Bottom view of a timing thermostat.

Fig. 7-7 shows an end view of a slightly different type of toaster. The same principle is used, but the timing is controlled by a small clockwork mechanism. When the rack is pushed down by hand, this clockwork is wound up and runs until the toast is done. Then, it trips the rack mechanism. This, too, is adjustable for darker or lighter toast.

THE SELF-LOWERING TOASTERS

Possibly the first of the fully automated self-lowering toasters was the Sunbeam. It uses a novel method of actuating the *lower-lift* mechanism. Fig. 7-8 shows a partial view of the unit

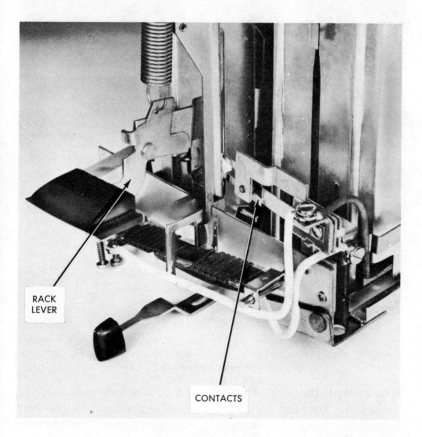

RACK
LEVER

CONTACTS

Fig. 7-6. Top view of the thermostat assembly shown in Fig. 7-5.

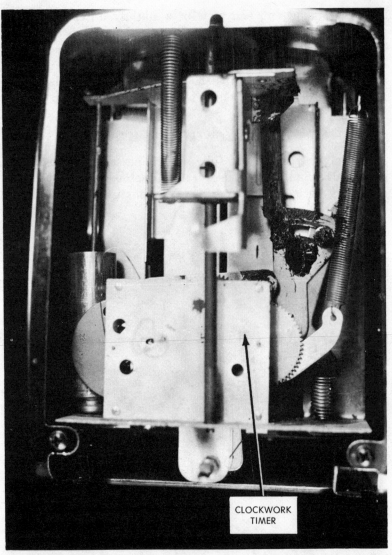

CLOCKWORK TIMER

Fig. 7-7. An automatic toaster with clockwork timer. When the rack is pushed down, the clockwork is wound up. It runs until the toast is ready, then trips the rack mechanism.

as seen with the case removed. Two rods are mounted on the right end; these are actually *U-shaped* and extend all the way around the case to the other side, which is exactly like the one shown.

The upper rod is fastened in a hole in the right end of the frame. The lower rod is movable; its end is fastened to a lever. At the left, a clamp holds a long arm which holds the bread racks. When the unit is off, the rods are in the up position as shown. When a slice of bread is dropped into the left slot and the power is off, nothing happens. Turning on the switch starts the cycle. This is what happens: The center heating element is wound on side frames made of a special alloy. When this element is heated, it *contracts*. Since the top of the center

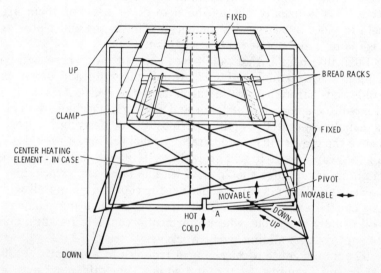

Fig. 7-8. A partial drawing of the self-lowering mechanism of a fully automatic toaster. When a slice of bread is placed in the left bread rack, the center heater element is actuated. After this is heated, it pulls up on lever "A," lowering the bread.

element is firmly fixed to the top of the frame, the contraction causes it to pull upward on the ends of the "A" levers. (There's one on the other side, too.) This leverage action causes a *pull* on the end of the lower rod, making the rods drop down, carrying the bread with them.

A timing thermostat controls the toasting time. The bread and racks stay down until the thermostat opens. When it does, the center element frames expand, pushing the lever down and making the rods rise (aided by a large, weak spring which was stretched when they went down). The heating elements are turned off. A trigger mechanism (not shown) cocks the thermostat; when another slice of bread is inserted, it's ready to start the cycle again.

SERVICING AUTOMATIC TOASTERS

An automatic toaster looks like a pretty complicated thing, and it is, mechanically. However, by being careful and by studying the action of the mechanism to find out "what does what," they're not too hard to fix! Take off the end plates or case. This is usually not too hard to do as most of them are held in place by screws on the bottom. When the end plates or case is off, you can see the mechanism.

Basically, here's what you'll see; check it out. There will be a light sheet-metal *bread rack,* which slides up and down on guide rods through holes in the ends of the racks. Attached to this will be some kind of latch and/or a trip mechanism. This is usually operated by the thermostat, as described before. Leave the power OFF, and carefully push the bread rack down all the way. See if it will stay there. If it won't, look for the latching device that should hold it. The latch isn't working.

Heating elements can be checked for continuity, and all wiring can be examined. Broken wires on the heating elements will usually be visible. Check thermostat contacts for dirt, and be sure that all sliding parts work very freely.

The major cause of mechanical troubles in automatic toasters is dirt—crumbs, butter, and so on. This will sometimes be *baked on* the slide rods, hinges, latches, and other moving parts, so that it interferes with their operation. The first step in any toaster-repair job should be a very careful but *thorough* cleanup!

When cleaning, be sure that you don't bend any of the slide rods, latches, or other delicate parts. A small paintbrush is very handy for getting accumulations of crumbs out of places. Blow them out of inaccessible places with a vacuum cleaner. If slide rods or guides are coated with a baked-on accumulation of grease, wash them carefully with some kind of solvent. If it's necessary, you can carefully scrape this off with the tip of a knife blade. Be sure that all sliding devices, hinges, latches, triggers, and other moving parts are completely free. In a lot of these units, especially the older ones, some of these things work by gravity—no springs. If there are springs, be sure that you don't stretch them while working around other parts.

Most parts of these toasters need very little or no lubrication. In certain places, you will have to lubricate to make the mechanism work properly. If so, do NOT use common household light oil. Since the whole mechanism gets pretty hot during use, the best lubricant is one of the heat-resisting types, such as Super-Moly, Moly-Kote, or another molybdenum compound. These are available at radio, tv, and appliance supply houses. Use lubricants *very sparingly*. Only a very thin coating is needed. Excess grease of any kind will catch and hold crumbs, dust, etc., and foul up the mechanism again in a short time.

If the mechanism of the toaster has been forced after a slight jam, you may find thin metal arms, etc., bent out of place. In most instances, you will be able to see how they *should* work, and bend them back. A pair of long-nose pliers is very useful for this kind of work. If the metal arms are badly bent, you can take them off and flatten them out again. Practically all of these are made of aluminum or thin sheet steel so that they're easy to *rework*. Cycle the mechanism several times, tripping it by hand. If it seems to be working all right, hook up the power, and run it through the normal toasting cycle. Be very careful while doing this since there is a definite shock hazard from the exposed heating elements. DON'T do this kind of work on a kitchen sink or around any grounded objects! Use a dry wooden workbench, and don't stand on a bare cement floor.

If the edges of latches, triggers, etc., have been worn or rounded off so that they won't latch properly, you can often "square them up" and make them hold by filing them with very small, specially shaped files called *pattern files*. A full set of these can be found in auto supply and hardware stores, and they are very handy for this kind of work.

HOT-DOG COOKER

Before we leave the *cooking* electrical appliances, let's look at a couple of really clever ones. The first is a *hot-dog cooker* made in the shape seen in Fig. 7-9. Along each side of the lower half are a row of spikes. The hot dogs are simply "impaled" on these as shown. There is a hinged lid, usually made of plastic. When the lid is lowered, the switch is closed, and the hot dogs cook. There is *no* heating element at all. How do the hot dogs cook, then? They develop their own heat, due to the electric current flowing through their moist interiors!

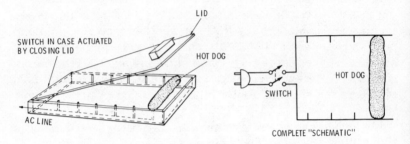

Fig. 7-9. A drawing of an electric hot-dog cooker. The switch is actuated by closing the lid. When a hot dog is placed on the spikes, current flows through the spike on one side, through the juices inside the hot dog, and through the spike on the other side.

The switch breaks both sides of the line. When the lid is open, there is no continuity between the two rows of spikes and the ac line. When the lid is closed, it pushes the hot dogs firmly down on the spikes and closes the switch. That's all!

BOTTLE WARMERS

An even simpler device is the automatic bottle warmer. This consists of a ceramic container, shaped something like a mug. The bottle is placed in this, and water is poured in. When the bottle warmer is plugged in, the bottle is warmed. Yet, there is no heating element! In the bottom of the container, you'll see a perforated ceramic disc. Take out the screw holding this, and you'll see only two small brass contacts connected to the ac line cord.

What makes the container get hot? The water itself provides the heat. If the container is dry when it's plugged in, nothing happens. When water is poured in, current flows between the two terminals. The resistance of the water develops enough heat to make the water hot. Incidentally, bottle warmers won't work at all with distilled water! Distilled water has no chemicals in it and won't pass an electric current.

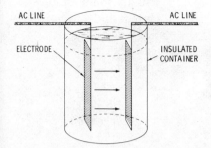

Fig. 7-10. This illustrates how water
is heated by using two electrodes.

Ordinary tap water always has enough chemicals in it to
provide a low resistance; this develops heat. The final temperature is determined by the amount of water used. The longer the
water boils, the hotter the bottle. When all of the water has
evaporated, the appliance turns itself off. Fig. 7-10 shows how
this works, and Fig. 7-11 shows one of these units with the
ceramic disc taken out. Repairs? If the line cord is broken, the
bottle warmer won't work. Only the line cord can be replaced,
because that's all there is!

Fig. 7-11. A bottle warmer with the
protective ceramic disc removed. The
two brass contacts are connected to
the ac line.

VAPORIZERS

Vaporizers, used for heating medicines to make soothing
vapors, work on the same principle as bottle warmers. Fig.
7-12 shows a vaporizer. This one has a removable *heating element,* which is just an insulated cup with two metal elements
inside. The insulated cup has holes in it so that the water can
get to the contacts. The cup is removable for cleaning and putting in the medication.

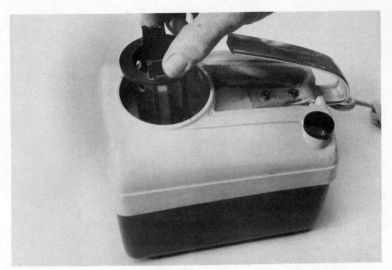

Fig. 7-12. Electric vaporizer with removable heating unit. Two metal elements are mounted on an insulated cup and can be removed for cleaning.

Fig. 7-13 shows the cup. The electrodes are the two closely spaced plates on the bottom. The contacts are the strips running up each side; these make contact with spring strips inside the case. The cup is made removable so that the greasy residue from the medication can be cleaned off. If the residue is thick enough, it could insulate the electrodes. In some localities, minerals in the water will leave a white chalky deposit on the electrodes. Normally, this won't hurt anything unless the deposit gets too thick. If it does, it can be scraped off.

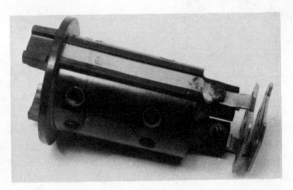

Fig. 7-13. Heating unit removed from the vaporizer.

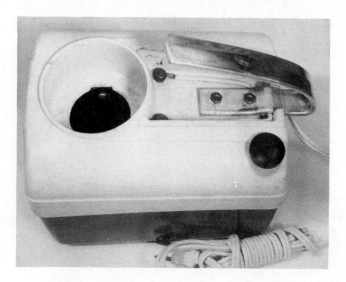

Fig. 7-14. Vaporizer with heating elements removed.

Repairs are the same as for the bottle warmer. If the vaporizer won't heat, the line cord is open. Check for an open cord at the plug and at the appliance.

Chapter 8

Modular Appliances

Everything is "going modular" these days, including electric appliances. One of the major appliance manufacturers, SCM/ Proctor-Silex, has been building a line of modular electric appliances that come in the more popular small units so common in the home. At this writing, these comprise four units: a two-slice automatic toaster, a combination toaster and table oven, an electric percolator, and, wonder of wonders, an electric iron. (This wonderment is because we found it extremely difficult to take apart some of the very first electric irons!)

All of these modular appliances are designed so that they can be completely disassembled, repaired, and put back together again without using even simple tools! The design is broken down into modules, which are held together by latches, clamps, etc., which can be taken apart with the fingers. The percolator is probably the simplest, so let's look at it first.

PERCOLATOR

This is a standard electric percolator. The unit is made in seven pieces as follows: the coffee basket-pump, lid, bowl, disc-plate, base, lamps, and cord. The heating element is a sealed type inside the plastic base. To take the base apart, take the lid off and open the bowl-release latch at the top of the handle (Fig. 8-1). Just lift the small cover, and the latch

Fig. 8-1. Illustrates removal of glass bowl. Grasp percolator handle near the top and push bowl away from the handle with your thumb while lifting bowl up and away with your other hand.

Courtesy Proctor-Silex Inc.

is right there. This should be done whenever the percolator is washed; the base shouldn't be immersed in water.

Power is supplied to the percolator through a standard cord and appliance plug. This, of course, will be the cause of most of the actual troubles if the unit won't heat. Check for the presence of ac at the sockets of the appliance plug with the test lamp or an ac voltmeter. If ac is normal, then check the heating element for continuity at the prongs inside the base. If the heating element shows an open circuit, the element should be replaced.

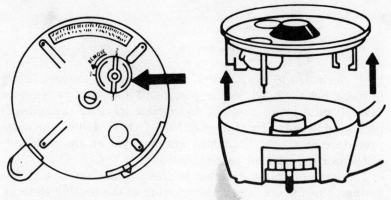

Courtesy Proctor-Silex Inc.

Fig. 8-2. Replacing the element. To remove the element, turn the base assembly upside down in the palm of your hand and turn the knob to Position "1"; next, turn the base assembly upright and lift out the element.

Replacing the element is simple. Turn the base assembly upside down (Fig. 8-2). You'll see a knob marked *1-2-3* and *closed*. Turn the knob to the position marked "1." Turn the unit over, and the disc-plate heating element can be lifted out. The thermostat is sealed inside the element assembly. To repair, replace this whole unit. The new unit will slip into the base; note the bracket which fits across the hole for the appliance plug. This is used to ensure that the element cannot be taken out unless the appliance plug has been removed. It is a safety feature; you can't get to a hot wire. To reassemble, turn the locking knob to Position "2." Set the new element so that the double prongs of the bracket are across the plug hole in the side of the base; you'll see the words *cord plug* on this bracket (Fig. 8-3). Slip it into place, and then turn the locking

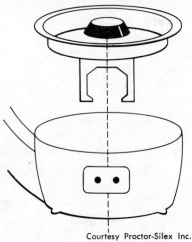

Fig. 8-3. To put in a new element, turn the knob to Position "2"; locate the double-pronged shaped bracket by the arrow and words cord plug; insert the element and press onto the base firmly; and turn the knob to Position "3."

Courtesy Proctor-Silex Inc.

knob clockwise to Position "3"; this locks the element firmly in place. Set the bowl back in place, and it's ready to use. Two 117-volt pilot lamps are used to indicate whether the coffee is perking or ready. To replace either of these, follow the same procedure as above; the lamps are mounted on the underside of the heating element assembly.

The bowl of this percolator is glass. There's a hole in the bottom; this fits over the round housing of the heating element. A gasket prevents leakage; if there is leakage from the base, this gasket is probably cracked. Get a new gasket; remove the bowl and replace the gasket, making certain that the gasket is set correctly and that the bowl fits tightly over it. Check the bottom of the bowl for cracked places or small chips out of the edge; either of these will cause leaks.

TOASTER

The toaster in this series is made in only five parts, one of which is the line cord and plug. The main *chassis* contains the heating elements, controls, and raising and lowering devices. The rest are the body, rear panel, and front panel, which has the crumb tray attached to it. This tray is hinged so that it can be let down to clean crumbs out of the toaster.

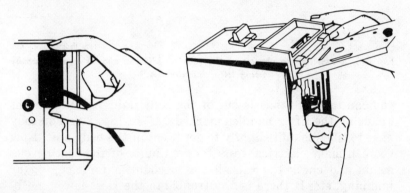

Courtesy Proctor-Silex Inc.

Courtesy Proctor-Silex Inc.

Fig. 8-4. To remove the line cord from the toaster, pull up on the large Bakelite plug at the end of the toaster.

Fig. 8-5. To remove the rear panel from the toaster, carefully tilt the base of panel away from toaster body and lift panel up and out.

Disassemble the toaster in the following manner: First, disconnect the line cord from the toaster by pulling up on the big Bakelite plug at the toaster end (take the plug out of the wall outlet first, of course!), as in Fig. 8-4. Next, turn the toaster upside down on a pad or soft cloth (to keep from scratching the case). Take out the front panel, which is the end with the color-selector control. Grasp this with your left hand and lift the release lever, conveniently marked *lift*, as you carefully tilt the base of the panel away from the body of the toaster. Lift the panel up and out, and it'll come loose. To take off the rear panel, do the same thing at the other end. Lift the lever to disengage it, then lift it up and away (Fig. 8-5). Now,

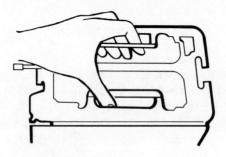

Courtesy Proctor-Silex Inc.

Fig. 8-6. Removing the chassis of the toaster. Lift the chassis straight up by using lifter handles "A."

you can take the chassis out of the body unit. Lift it straight up, using the lifter handles marked "A" in Fig. 8-6. You may have to tilt this unit slightly to get it out of the body unit. Now you can make electrical tests for continuity of the heating elements and check the raise-lower mechanism for clogging or jamming, etc. If there is any trouble in the raise-lower mechanism, it is recommended that the chassis unit be replaced. It isn't intended to be repaired.

To reassemble, reverse this procedure. Place the body unit upside down on the pad. The front end will be marked with a red mark and the word *front* printed on the top flange. Turn the chassis unit upside down and look for another red mark which indicates the front end. Holding the bottom of the chassis by the handles as before, slide it into the body unit, guiding the top center of the chassis into the channel between the toaster-well openings (where the bread slices go). Be sure that you have the red marks on both units at the same corner. You'll see a small locking tab and socket on each corner of the unit. These must go all the way down and lock tightly into the small square sockets in the body of the toaster (Fig. 8-7).

Replace the panel marked *rear* next (Fig. 8-8). Find the rear of the toaster body; it will be opposite the end with the color-selector control and marked with the word *rear*. Hold this

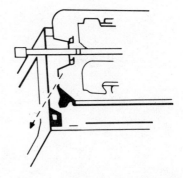

Fig. 8-7. To reassemble the chassis in the toaster, locate the front end of the toaster body which has a red mark near the base. Locate the front end of the chassis which has a red mark at the corner. Grasp the chassis by handles and insert it into the toaster body, mating the red corner of the chassis with the red hole in the body. Make sure the tabs go all the way down and lock firmly into the square-shaped socket holes.

Courtesy Proctor-Silex Inc.

panel in the palm of your hand, with the release lever at the top. Slide the metal locking tab into the notch at the end of the top of the body, then press it firmly into place. Tilt this panel in and down toward the body until it snaps shut; it'll latch automatically and hold.

Next, pick up the panel marked *front;* set the color selector lever on the chassis in the middle position. Set this in place

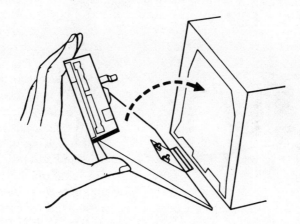

Courtesy Proctor-Silex Inc.

Fig. 8-8. The rear panel is marked rear and the word rear is stamped into the body of the toaster. To replace this rear panel, hold the panel in the palm of your hand with the release lever at the top. Place metal locking tab "A" into notch "B" and press firmly into place. Tilt the panel in and down toward the body until it snaps shut.

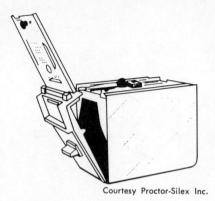

Courtesy Proctor-Silex Inc.

Fig. 8-9. The front panel is marked front and the word front is stamped into the body of the toaster. To replace the front panel, position color selector on the chassis in the center position. Place the metal locking tab into the notch and tilt the front panel toward the chassis guiding selector lever "A" through the slot in the panel.

just as you did the rear panel. When you tilt the front panel toward the chassis, be sure that the color-selector lever goes through the slot in the panel; Fig. 8-9 shows how this goes. With the front panel in place, close the crumb tray and push down on its knob to latch it.

Finally, insert the Bakelite cord plug into the hole in the rear panel and push it into place. Turn the toaster right side up; grasp the lifter knob, as in Fig. 8-10. Raise this up as far as it will go, then lower it as far as possible and raise it again. The operating machinery is now connected.

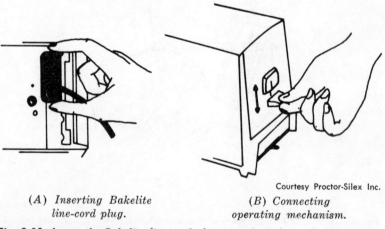

Courtesy Proctor-Silex Inc.

(A) *Inserting Bakelite*
line-cord plug.

(B) *Connecting*
operating mechanism.

Fig. 8-10. Insert the Bakelite line-cord plug into the hole in the rear panel. After turning the toaster upright, grasp lifter knob "A" and raise it up as far as it will go, then lower it as far as it will go and raise it again. The operating mechanism is now connected.

Troubleshooting on modular toasters is the same as on the other models discussed in the section on toasters. If it won't heat up at all, check to make sure that the line cord is good and that the heating elements aren't burned out. If the toaster heats up but the pop-up mechanism isn't working properly, check the pop-up mechanism for any sign of binding. The lifter knob must slide freely over the full length of the slot in the panel. If it does not, find out what is bent. The panel may be damaged; if so, it can be replaced with a new one without trouble.

COMBINATION TOASTER AND TABLE OVEN

Next in this series we find a combination toaster and table oven unit. This unit uses four sealed plug-in heating elements. These can be replaced one at a time if necessary. It looks like a conventional table oven with a door on the front; however, on top you'll see two slots like those in a standard toaster. The unit will toast two slices at once. If only one slice is wanted, be sure that it's placed in the slot at the *right* end of the unit, as you face it.

Two sets of controls are used. On the right end are the controls for the toaster; this includes a color selector for light or dark toast and the lifter knob. On the left side of the panel are the controls for the oven, including a temperature-control thermostat marked in degrees. The unit can't be used for both purposes at the same time; it's either a toaster or an oven.

Disassembly

To take this appliance apart for servicing or testing, take out the oven tray. To take out the oven rack, lift up the front to unhook the back locks, then pull straight out. The crumb tray, which is under this, can be taken out by lifting the front edge and pulling forward (Fig. 8-11). Now, stand the unit on its left end and pull the large plug from its socket on the underside of the case (Fig. 8-12).

To take the toaster control panel off, push down on the end of the case and slide the latch in the *unlock* direction, toward the back of the case (Fig. 8-13). When this releases, lift the bottom edge of the panel up and slide it toward you to release the panel clip from the top of the case (Fig. 8-14).

The sockets and one end of the four plug-in heating elements will now be uncovered. Each element is a rod which slides into a hole in what is now the top end of the case and plugs into a socket on the other end. To remove these elements, pull them straight up and out (Fig. 8-15). They can now be tested for continuity, and any open units can be replaced.

(A) Removing oven rack.

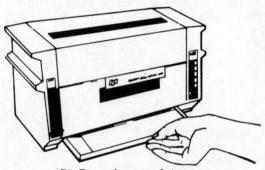

(B) Removing crumb tray.

Courtesy Proctor-Silex Inc.

Fig. 8-11. Illustrates the oven rack and crumb tray removal. To remove oven rack, lift up the front of the rack. This disengages the back locks and permits the rack to be pulled out. The crumb tray is removed by pulling forward on it.

To replace the heating elements, slide them back through the hole in the right end (case still standing on the left end as before) and into the corresponding holes in the other end. By opening the oven door, it is easy to guide them into place (Fig. 8-16).

To replace the control panel, check to be sure that the latch is in the *unlocked* position. Slide the clip on the panel under the

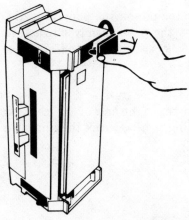

Fig. 8-12. Stand the appliance up on its left end (place a soft cloth under it) and pull out the line-cord plug.

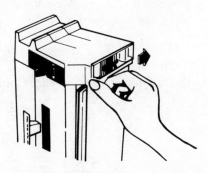

Fig. 8-13. To unlock the control panel, press down on the control panel and move the slide latch toward the rear of the appliance, as indicated by arrow.

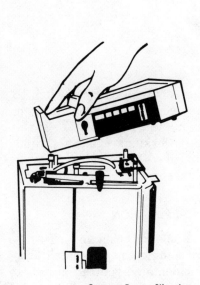

Fig. 8-14. To remove the control panel, lift the bottom of the panel up and slide the panel down until it disengages from the body of the appliance.

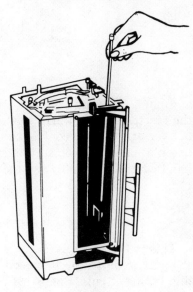

Fig. 8-15. To remove the four heating elements, pull each one straight up and out of the appliance.

flange on the body. Guide the locator pin on the panel into the matching hole in the body. Press the panel firmly down into place and slip the latch back to *lock* position (Fig. 8-17). Replace the line cord and plug.

Troubleshooting

The master on-off switch is on the right end of the case on the toaster control panel. If nothing works, check the line cord

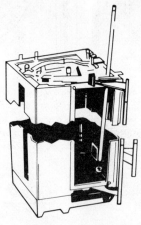

Fig. 8-16. To replace the elements, open the oven door and insert each element in the round hole in the end of the appliance and guide it into the corresponding hole in the opposite end of the appliance.

Courtesy Proctor-Silex Inc.

and plug, and then take the panel off to check this switch. If the toaster section works but the oven section won't, turn the OVEN TEMPERATURE control to its highest point, 500° F. If this doesn't make the oven section start working, replace the right-hand control panel. To use the toaster, the oven tray must be removed. The tray will stop the toaster rack from latching.

THE STEAM/DRY/SPRAY IRON

This is the one I like! It's so simple it's marvelous. To take it apart, remove the line cord by sliding the plug latch away and lifting it out (Fig. 8-18). Incidentally, you can do this to make the iron easier to use for a right-handed or left-handed person. Next, take off the handle and the water reservoir. You'll see a release knob on the end of a lever, under the plastic water reservoir on the left side of the iron. Slide the release knob toward the front of the iron, as in Fig. 8-19. Lift the

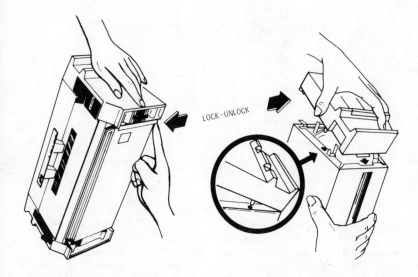

LOCK - UNLOCK

Fig. 8-17. Replacing the control panel. With the latch in the unlocked position, tilt the control panel and insert the clip on the panel under the flange on the body of the appliance. Guide the locating pin on the panel into the hole in the body, and press down firmly on the panel, moving the slide latch to the lock position.

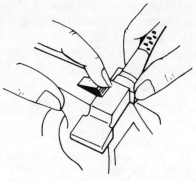

Fig. 8-18. To remove the iron cord assembly, slide cord plug latch "3" away from the cord assembly and lift up on the assembly.

Fig. 8-19. Remove the handle and reservoir from the soleplate. Lift release lever knob "5" and slide it to full release position "5A." Grasp the handle and pull it away from the soleplate.

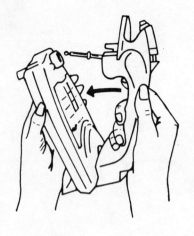

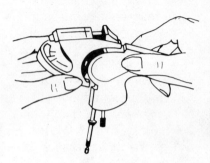

Fig. 8-20. Remove the handle from reservoir. Grasp the handle in one hand and the reservoir in the other hand. Press the reservoir down firmly toward the rear of the handle and pull the front or top of the reservoir gently away from the handle.

Fig. 8-21. Removing the spray pump and filler subassembly from the handle. Grasp the handle in one hand, the spray filler subassembly in the other hand. Lift the spray filler subassembly up and away from the handle until it disengages from the handle.

knob up a short way at first, then move it all the way to the front. Now you can take the handle and tank off by simply lifting them up and away from the soleplate unit.

To get the reservoir off the handle unit, hold the handle in your right hand, front end of iron up. Now, grasp the reservoir unit in your left hand and push down firmly toward the back of the handle. The front (top) of the reservoir can then be

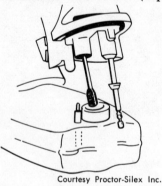

Fig. 8-22. Reassemble the handle and reservoir to the soleplate assembly. Reassembly should be done in the reverse order of disassembly, as illustrated in Figs. 8-21, 8-20, and 8-19. Make sure everything is lined up properly.

pulled (carefully!) away from the handle (Fig. 8-20). The spray pump and filler subassembly can now be disengaged from the front of the handle, as in Fig. 8-21. Lift them up and away from the handle unit.

To reassemble, simply reverse these steps. When putting the reservoir, handle unit, and soleplate back together, be careful not to let the little pipes, etc., get out of place. Fig. 8-22 shows how they must go into the opening in the soleplate. Don't use force; when you get everything properly lined up, they'll all slip into place without any problems. With everything all put back together, set the units on the soleplate, making sure that the lever is in the *forward* (open) position. Finally, set the iron down and move the lever to the back until the lever is against the handle, out of the way. Put the cord on, and the job is done.

Chapter **9**

Portable Electric Heaters

Electric heaters, usually called *space heaters,* come in many shapes and sizes, but as we've said before, they're all basically alike. The simplest types have nothing but a heating element and line cord, in a metal cabinet with grilles to allow the heat to get out. A more versatile model adds an adjustable thermostat to control the heat and sometimes act as an on-off switch. From this model, we go to heaters having small fans in the cabinets to blow the hot air wherever needed. Most of these types will have multiple heating elements so that you can select the heat, for example, medium, warm, or hot.

All of the heating-element types previously mentioned are found in space heaters. Perhaps the majority now use either coiled-wire or flat-wire types. There is one type of special heating element used in some which isn't found in other appliances. It looks like a frosted glass rod; it isn't. It's made of a special compound which has fairly low resistance. When the line voltage is connected to the ends, the rod gets hot.

Fig. 9-1 shows the heating element and fan of a typical unit with the bottom cover removed. Fig. 9-2 shows the thermostat used in this unit.

HEATER REPAIRS

There is no doubt about diagnosing the trouble in an electric heater, and it is generally easy to repair. Check the line cord and plug first, as for all other appliances. Many of these use a *heater cord*, which is a braid-covered standard of wire wrapped with asbestos, like the type used on electric irons. Others use heavy rubber-coated cord like that used on tv sets. Check to see that the wire is not broken inside the insulation near the wall plug; this is the most common trouble. To make sure, take off one side of the cover, plug it in, and check for the presence of ac voltage at the ends of the line cord; use the little neon tester. If there is voltage at this point but the ele-

Fig. 9-1. The fan and heating elements of a typical electric heater. This heater uses a coil-spring element; others use flat-wire elements wound on a mica card, and some have sealed elements like those on an electric range.

ment will not heat, check through the thermostat. Fig. 9-3 shows how to do this. If there is voltage at the *line* side of the thermostat but none at the *load* side, the thermostat is not making contact. If there is voltage at the load side of the thermostat but the element will not heat, it is definitely open. If your heater has coiled-spring elements, breaks are easy to see. The wire will fall off the supports.

Fig. 9-2. This illustrates the thermostat of a typical electric heater. The fan motor is mounted on a bracket in the center.

A broken element should be replaced with a new one. If it has been in service long enough to break (caused mostly by corrosion of the heater wire from repeated heating and cooling), the rest of the wire will be brittle and will break again

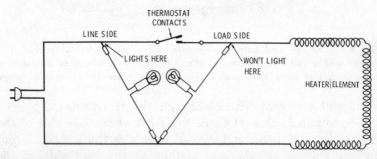

Fig. 9-3. Method of checking the thermostatic contacts on an electric heater. If there is voltage at the line side of the thermostat but none at the load side, the thermostat is not making contact. If there is voltage at the load side of the thermostat but the element will not heat, the element is open.

soon. Cleaning off the broken ends and twisting them tightly together will make an emergency repair, but this kind of joint will not last. It will oxidize and break again very shortly. However, this is a good way to keep it going until you can get a replacement element. *Caution:* The exposed-wire type of heating element (like the one shown) is dangerous. Whenever you touch these wires, be sure that the line plug is pulled out and lying where you can see it. You can get a very bad shock from the wires. If the heater has been turned off for only a moment, you can get a painful burn from touching the wires.

Replacement Elements

You can get replacement elements in whatever size you need at any electrical supply store. Look at the rating plate of your heater; it will give you the information needed to get an exact duplicate. The coiled elements which you get will be a lot shorter than the original, but they will be the same *electrical* size. To install one of these elements, fasten the two ends and then very carefully stretch the element over and around the ceramic insulating supports. Do not overdo this, because the element must have enough *spring* left to hold it tightly on the supports. The wires are bare and must *never* be allowed to touch or even come close to the metal of the case. If the element touches the metal of the case, you will get a very dangerous shock.

If you accidentally stretch the element too far, you can sometimes bring it back by pushing the coils back together between your fingers. If it is still slack, tie the element to the ceramic supports with bits of small, bare wire. If you can see a place where the element might touch the case, glue a piece of sheet asbestos to the case under the element. The kind used to cover furnace pipes, etc., will do nicely.

Connections

Many of the older heaters used screw terminals. The newer models use push-on terminals, like those found in your automobile wiring. Fig. 9-4 shows the new element support. Ceramic pins hold the heating element in place, and the element ends have *crimped-on* terminals which connect to resistance wire. You can get these terminals at garages or most radio-parts supply stores. If you get a factory replacement element made by the original manufacturer of your heater the new element may come with the terminals already mounted. To install one of these crimp-on terminals, scrape the end of the element wire very clean, push it into the end of the connector, and then crimp it tightly with a pair of small pliers. Crush the sleeve end of the connector until you can be sure that it is making a very good, tight connection. Pull on it to be sure

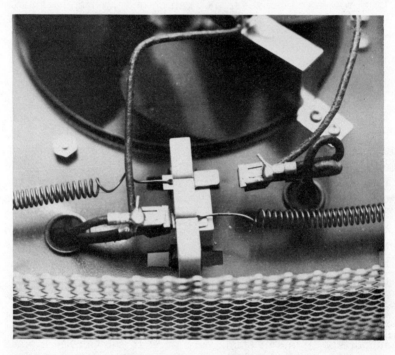

Fig. 9-4. A typical connector block used on electric heaters. Ceramic pins hold the heating element in place, and the element ends have crimped-on terminals which connect to resistance wire.

there is no slack or looseness. To make a tight connection of a small wire in a large connector, double the bare end of the wire to fill up the hole in the end of the connector, then crimp.

On ordinary wires (motor, line cord, etc.) the same type of connectors is used, but these can be soldered if necessary. In fact, you can see a small blob of solder on the motor wire in Fig. 9-4. If the female connectors are loose on the blades of the male units, very carefully pinch them between the jaws of the

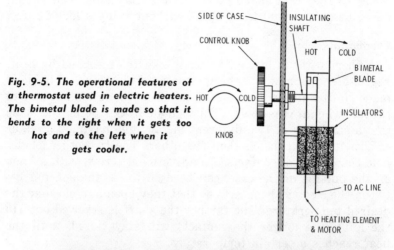

Fig. 9-5. The operational features of a thermostat used in electric heaters. The bimetal blade is made so that it bends to the right when it gets too hot and to the left when it gets cooler.

Fig. 9-6. A closeup view of a thermostat control on an electric heater. To clean the contacts, cut a strip of fine sandpaper about ½-inch wide. Fold the paper so the sandy surface is on both sides. Open the contacts and pull the sandpaper back and forth through the contacts while holding them together.

115

pliers so that they make good, tight connections. You should never be able to pull them apart without using a lot of force.

Thermostats

A thermostat is just an automatic switch operated by heat. Fig. 9-5 shows how the thermostat works. A *bimetal* blade is made so that it bends to the right when it gets too hot and to the left when it gets cooler. This is done by designing the blade into a sandwich of two different metals, one having a greater coefficient of expansion than the other. The two other blades hold the electrical contacts. An adjustment screw, with a knob on the outside of the case, can be used to set the spacing between the electrical contacts so that they open and close at the desired temperature. The farther the shaft is screwed out (to the left), the longer the contacts will stay closed, until the heat reaches a certain temperature.

To check the thermostat, use the neon tester as mentioned before. Look at the contacts; they may be dark in color, but they should be smooth-surfaced. If they are rough and pitted, they will not make very good contact and should be cleaned. Fig. 9-6 shows a close-up of the thermostat on the heater shown in Fig. 9-1. The contacts in this model are easy to service, but others may have to be loosened and removed to allow cleaning and adjustment. To clean the thermostat contacts, cut a strip of fine sandpaper about ½ inch wide the full length of the sheet. Fold the strip of paper so that the sanding surface is on both sides. Open the contacts and push the sandpaper through. Hold the contacts together and pull the sandpaper back and forth. Repeat this until the surface of the contacts is smooth and bright. Finish off by cutting a strip from a piece of cardboard, such as an old postcard, and pull this through to give the surfaces a high polish. Cardboard is just rough enough to smooth down surfaces like this very nicely.

Check the setting of the thermostat knob to be sure that it will let the contacts close tightly. A loose contact can *chatter* and cause arcing. This will make the contacts burn up again in a short time and you will have your cleaning job to do over. Check all wire terminal connections to be sure that they are not loose. Loose connections in heavy-current circuits like this will get very hot, burn up, and possibly cause other serious trouble.

Switches

Some of these heaters will be equipped with *tip switches.* These are safety switches which cut the current off if the heater is accidentally knocked over. A metal rod comes out of the bottom of the case and touches the floor. When the heater is sitting in its normal position, the rod is pushed up inside the case and holds a switch closed. If the heater is turned over, a spring pushes the rod down, opening the switch. This is handy, for a radiant heater like this could burn a large hole in a carpet or tile and can even set a wooden floor on fire if the heater happened to be turned face down.

Fan Motors

The fan motor can be seen in Fig. 9-2. The motors used in these heaters are small induction-type motors with solid rotors and are practically trouble-free. They very seldom need oiling. Turn the fan blade with your fingers; if it spins freely, the fan does not need oil. If the blade *drags,* put one drop of oil on each

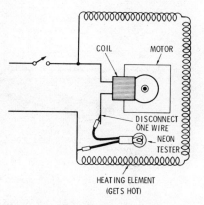

Fig. 9-7. Testing for an open motor coil with a neon tester. With the neon tester connected from the open motor wire to the other side of the ac line, turn the heater on. If the lamp glows, the motor coil is good.

motor bearing, and run the motor until it comes back up to normal speed. One drop is enough, for you have only two very small bearings to oil. Too much oil will drip off, and it will get onto the heater element and cause an obnoxious smell.

Turn the heater on, and check with the neon lamp from the open motor wire to the other side of the ac line as shown in Fig. 9-7. If the lamp glows, the motor coil isn't open. If the lamp doesn't glow but the heating element gets hot, the motor coil is open. If the heater works, voltage is getting to the unit.

If the lamp glows but the motor will not run, the rotor is probably stuck from lack of oil or from lint or dust in the frame. This is easy to see. Clean out the space inside the motor frame, put in a drop of oil, and spin the rotor with your fingers until it is free. If the fan rattles while running, look for loose bolts in the mounting or loose blades, etc. Some fans are fastened to the motor shaft by setscrews through the hub. If these work loose, then the fan will vibrate and make noises.

BEAUTY-CARE APPLIANCES

Hair curlers and hair setters are two popular hair-setting appliances that have heating devices.

Hair Curlers

One old unit which has made a comeback recently is the "curling iron." Cleopatra is shown using one of these in old Egyptian paintings! However, we've improved it a bit; it's

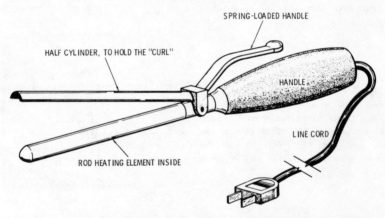

Fig. 9-8. A typical electric hair curler. The heating element is a sealed type inside the cylinder. Most of the trouble will be in the line cord.

now electrically heated. (When the writer was a tad, a curling iron was heated by dropping it down the chimney of a kerosene lamp!) Fig. 9-8 shows the inside of a curling iron. The heating element is a sealed type inside the cylinder. The elements are fairly low-wattage types. In many units, the whole rod must be replaced if the element opens. Most of the troubles, as usual, will be line cords that are broken due to constant flexing.

Hair Setters

The "setters" and similar appliances are sold under a multitude of trade names, but they all operate on the same principle. After shampooing, the hair is rolled up on toothed plastic rollers and pinned in place. If these are warm, the hair dries quicker. So, many of these are made with aluminum cores. The rollers come in three sizes: small, medium, and large.

The rollers are heated by being dropped over rods mounted on a metal plate, as in Fig. 9-9. The plate has a heating element mounted beneath it. Most hair setters have adjustable thermostats so that the rollers can be used at whatever temperature is desired.

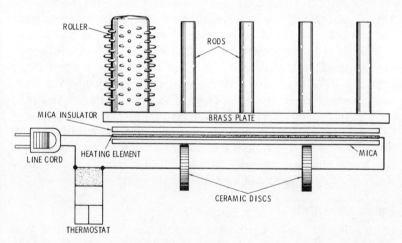

Fig. 9-9. A typical electric hair setter. The heating element is mounted underneath. The temperature in most hair setters is thermostatic controlled.

In the second version, the heat is carried to the rollers by steam. The basic construction of the device is the same, but there are no rods to carry the heat. The case is made like a shallow tray of plastic. The bottom is a metal plate with a thermostat-controlled heating element below it. A tightly fitting transparent plastic cover holds the steam in until the rollers are warm enough. The dampness makes the hair "take a set" more easily. Most steam models use a perforated plastic grid in the bottom to keep the rollers from touching the heating element.

Here, too, there are a great many variations; most steam hair setters can be used as "moisturizers" by taking out the rollers and adding some soothing lotion to the hot water. Plastic hoods, etc., are used to guide the steam to the face.

Checking and Repair

A curler or a setter has only a heating element, thermostat, and line cord. These usually aren't handled as roughly as those of other appliances, so line cords should last longer. Thermostats can get dirty and refuse to make contact, or the heating element can open. These normally use flat-type elements from 300 to 500 watts. Most of them are wrapped on a mica *card* like a toaster element. Both sides of the element must be very well insulated if the unit is the metal plate with rods type. After making any repairs, be sure to check for any electrical leakage between the element and any exposed metal parts.

Most of these units will be in plastic cases. Polyethylene and similar plastics are the most popular. If these are cracked or broken so that they leak water, they can be repaired with common plastic cement, such as Duco Household Cement and others. Metal parts, if broken, can be straightened up and repaired with cyanoacrylate cement, which sets in only a few seconds. This is found under names like Oneida's Instant-Weld. Don't use this for polyethylene and Teflon plastics. For anything else, cyanoacrylate cement is all right.

Taking Them Apart

In a lot of these units and similar appliances, you'll find small hex nuts down in the bottom of hex-shaped holes in the case. These can be tricky. To get them out, simply unscrew the screws from the top until you hear the nuts fall out. After taking out all of the screws, the case will come apart easily, exposing the heating elements, thermostat, and wiring.

Putting the unit back together is something else. Put a screw in the hole, then drop the nut into the hole, with the case upside down. If you're lucky, it won't turn sidewise! If things go as they usually do, it will. There are two ways to make this easier. The first way is to slip the nut onto a piece of thin wire, put the screw in, then put the end of the wire on the end of the screw. Now, let go of the nut, and it'll slide down the wire and go into the hole like it should. Turn the screw until the nut is caught. In any appliance like this, be sure that all of the screws are started before you tighten any of them! If you don't, sure enough, the last hole won't be lined up, and you'll have to loosen all of the others. It never fails to happen. The second method is to put a tiny dab of wax, etc., on the end of a toothpick, match, etc., and stick the nut to this.

Chapter 10

Electric Blankets and Heating Pads

BLANKETS

The electric blanket has a flexible heating element sewed right into the material and covering almost the entire area, as seen in Fig. 10-1. A thermostat keeps the temperature constant at the preselected level. In simpler versions the control is merely a thermostat, a pilot light (usually a tiny neon bulb), or an on-off switch sometimes incorporated in the thermostat-control knob.

Some blankets have dual controls and two separate heating elements (Fig. 10-2), one for each half of the bed. Thus, the temperature can be individually regulated for each side.

The blanket control box contains an adjustable thermostat with a magnetic contact—a common device in these controls. Fig. 10-3 shows how it works. The lower contact is fixed to the base plate and is surrounded by a small iron washer. Attached to the upper contact arm is a small, cup-shaped magnet (which does *not* make electrical contact in any way).

As the thermostat bends the arm, the magnet gets closer and closer to the fixed contact. Without the magnets, the contact points would come together very slowly until they made contact; this would result in a certain amount of sparking, and the contact would not be firm. By use of the magnets, however,

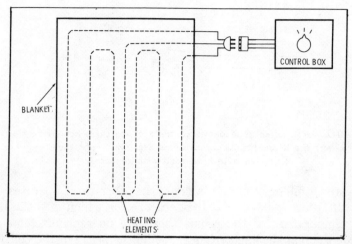

Fig. 10-1. *The heating element arrangement in a single control electric blanket. The temperature is thermostatic controlled by the control box.*

the contacts, when within a certain distance of each other, snap together and make a quick, firm contact. The same action occurs, only in reverse, on a break—the magnets hold the contacts together until the pull of the heating thermostat overcomes the magnetic attraction, and the contacts snap apart.

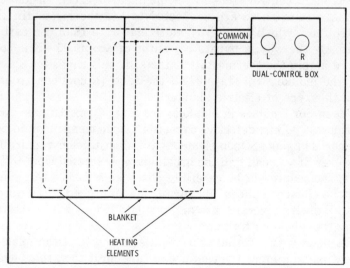

Fig. 10-2. *The heating element arrangement in a dual-control electric blanket. Either side can be controlled independently of the other.*

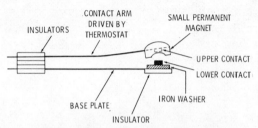

Fig. 10-3. Construction of magnetic contacts. When these are driven close to each other, the magnetic attraction takes over and snaps them together to provide a firm contact instantaneously.

In the simpler electric blankets, the thermostat operates on the difference between the temperature for which it is set and the temperature of the room; there are no sensing elements inside the blanket itself. Hence, should the user put the control unit *under* the electric blanket, the thermostat would not readily sense room-temperature changes. The control box must be set on a night table or the floor, never in the bed. (One poor soul dropped her control box out of bed, and it landed on top of a small night light near the floor. The temperature of the night-light bulb kept the blanket shut off all night!)

In some of the more elaborate blankets using what is called "electronic" control, sensing elements are placed inside the blanket itself. These are connected to the thermostat in the control box, which is slightly more elaborate than the earlier types. By the way, a bypass capacitor of about .05 uF is connected across the thermostat contacts; if this capacitor shorts out, the blanket will stay on all the time (a common trouble with this type of electric blanket).

The major troubles in blankets are control-box defects, dirty thermostat points, defective capacitors, open elements, and bad line cords or plugs. Open elements are almost never repairable. However, if you can find the break and it is located close to the edge, the seams can be carefully slit open with a razor blade and the element spliced. Be sure to make a good, tight joint; wrap the wire several times and insulate it well with asbestos, tying the whole with thread.

Blankets with internal thermostats can be tested by placing a heating pad under the center and turning it to various heats while watching the action of the control thermostat. This same procedure is also handy for checking the simpler control boxes.

(If it is summer and the room isn't cool enough to lower the temperature to the point where the blanket will turn on, try holding the box in front of an air-conditioner outlet. If none is available, wrap a few ice cubes in a cloth and place under the box.)

HEATING PADS

Heating pads are very similar to electric blankets, but have no control box. The standard pad provides three heats controlled by a selector switch. One resistance element gives a low heat, another a medium heat, and both are connected when high heat is desired. A cable-type wafer, rotary, or push-button switch allows the user to select the desired temperature. Most pads use very small thermostats in series with the heating elements. These are a constant source of trouble in the older models and even in some of the newer ones. In some makes they can be replaced by ripping a seam at one edge of the pad, opening the cover, and cutting out the defective thermostat. The repair procedure is the same as for electric blankets; make a tight, well-insulated joint in order to prevent a shock hazard to the user.

Chapter 11

Lighting and Controls

Various types of lighting and lighting controls are being used in homes today. This chapter discusses three-way lamps, fluorescent lamps, photoelectric light controls, and solid-state light dimmers. It describes how they work, how to troubleshoot them when they are not working, and how to repair them.

THREE-WAY LAMPS

Three-way lamps are found, in one version or another, in almost all homes. They can be table or floor lamps with two or more bulbs that can be switched on one at a time or all at once. A standard sequence for these would be "1," "2," 'both," and then off (Fig. 11-1). Some versions use a three-way bulb with 100-200-300-watt filaments. Other versions use single bulbs and selector switches.

To find the trouble, make sure that all the bulbs are good. This is easy—just screw a bulb that is known to be good into the suspected socket. If it is a bad switch, one particular bulb will refuse to light or will light every other time the switch is turned to that position. Bad switches will usually become very noisy; the bulb will flicker on and off, and you will hear a loud noise in the radio or television. The switches themselves are not easy to repair. A contact is usually burned up from long use, and, in any case, the construction of the switch makes it difficult to take apart and put back together. The best way

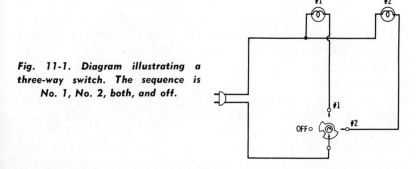

to correct this situation is to install a new switch, which is inexpensive and provides much better service.

To repair a bad switch, take the switch housing apart. Fig. 11-2 shows a typical lamp, opened and ready for checking. There will be two or three small screws holding the switch housing together. The wires will be tucked down inside the body of the lamp. Pull them up and separate the wires so that

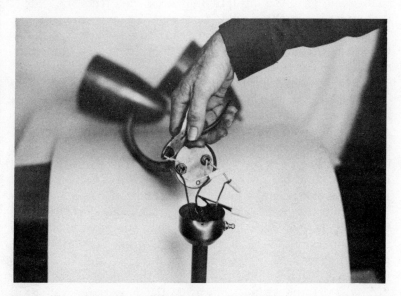

Fig. 11-2. A typical three-way lamp with the selector switch exposed. To replace the switch, unscrew the wire nuts and separate the wires. If the wires on the new switch haven't been stripped, strip them back about ¼ inch. Twist the ends together and put the wirenuts back on.

you can see which ones go to the switch. They should be fastened together with wire nuts, which are solderless connectors made especially for this kind of work. To take one apart, simply hold the wires near the wire nut and unscrew it, going counterclockwise. You will see that the ends of the wires are twisted together; untwist them and pull them apart. You will also notice that one wire from the line cord goes to the wires going up to the lamps. This is the *common* wire, and it does not go through the switch. Leave this alone; you do not have to bother it. Taking hold of the loose switch wires, unscrew the knurled nut holding the switch on the lamp. Use a pair of small gas-pliers to loosen the nut and remove the old switch.

You can get replacement switches at any electrical-appliance dealer's store. If you have any doubt, take the old switch with you so that you will be sure to get one with the right number of positions, etc. Put the new switch in, and tighten it well so that the body of the switch will not turn when you turn the lamp on and off. Bring the wire leads up and out so that you can get at them to make the connections. To make this kind of connection, strip the insulation about ¼ inch from the ends of the wires. Twist the strands clockwise. The wires on the new switch will already be stripped ready to hook up. In order to get the best connection, the other wires should be clipped off neatly to make new ends.

Hold the wires together, going the same way, and twist the ends clockwise a couple of times. Put the open end of the wire nut over the ends of the wires, and tighten it by turning it clockwise until you feel it tighten up. Be very sure that the insulation of the wires goes up into the end of the wire nut so that there are no bare wires showing at all. You need only about ¼ inch of bare wire to make this connection. If you have more than this, clip the end off with a pair of cutters.

Make up the other connections in the same way, and plug the lamp in and check it. Be sure that you have good bulbs. Ordinarily, you will have it hooked up right. The case of the new switch will be marked "L" for *line*, "1" and "2" for the two lamps. Be sure that the wire from the line cord goes to the "L" wire on the switch; however, the bulb wires can go to either one. If this should be a pole lamp with three separate bulbs, they originally lit up from the top down. You may have to change one or two of the bulb wires to get it back in the original order. On the two-lamp units, it does not make a great deal of difference which is "1" or "2."

If your lamp has the solid-metal shades, you may have trouble with the lamp sockets overheating. If there is not enough ventilation or if oversize bulbs are used, the sockets or wiring can suffer from heat deterioration. They are not hard to replace; each socket is held by a knurled nut at the top, like the switch. Always use replacement sockets made out of ceramic or heat-resistant plastic. Watch out for wires with rubber insulation. If the wiring is old and has been over-heated, the insulation will crack and fall off as the lamp is moved around. This can cause a dangerous short circuit, blowing the fuse. Also, one of the wires may contact the base of the lamp, which could cause a fatal electric shock.

When you are working on these lamps, *always* check the condition of the wiring. If it is old, frayed, or the insulation is very brittle, do not take any chances. Replace all wiring with new wires, and be sure to use wire with asbestos or fiber glass insulation. Get stranded wire so that it will hold up under constant bending and flexing, which it will get when the lamp is moved around and adjusted.

FLUORESCENT LIGHTS

Fluorescent lights are wired the same as incandescent lights. However, the lamps used require an automatic *starter* unit and a special *ballast* unit in series with the bulb. The ballast unit is simply an iron-core coil in a housing. There will be two wires coming out of it. These are not polarized; hook them up either way. The basic circuit of this type of fluorescent lamp is shown in Fig. 11-3.

Fig. 11-4 shows one end of a small fluorescent lamp; you can see the starter, which plugs into a socket, and one of the two sockets for the lamp itself. Wire nuts are used to make the connections to each part. The ballast is out of sight in this photo, but it will be a black-painted unit bolted to the frame of the lamp.

Some of the later models of this type use a special type of lamp that lights instantly. No starter is needed with this type. However, when you replace one of these lamps, be sure that you use the same type found in the original.

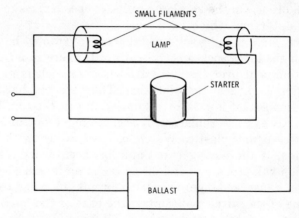

SMALL FILAMENTS

LAMP

STARTER

BALLAST

Fig. 11-3. The basic circuit of a fluorescent lamp. If the lamp flickers but refuses to flash on, the starter is probably bad. If the lamp doesn't flicker, the bulb is probably bad or the ballast is probably open.

In general, if a fluorescent lamp flickers on and off but refuses to flash on, the starter is probably bad. A starter can cause most of this kind of trouble. If the lamp still won't light, try a new bulb. If the ballast unit is open, the lamp won't even flicker. Check it for continuity. It should show a small amount of resistance. If the ballast must be replaced, check the wat-

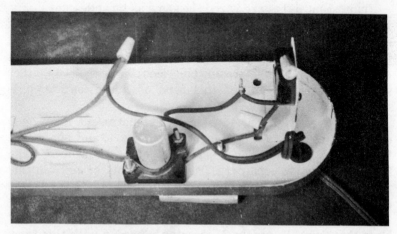

Fig. 11-4. One end of a small fluorescent lamp. Wire nuts such as these are often used to secure a splice. The two wires to be joined are twisted together as shown, and the wire nut is screwed over the connection, holding it securely.

tage of the lamp. For example, if you have a 20-watt fluorescent lamp, you'll need a 20-watt ballast to go with it. If the fixture has two or more lamps, special ballasts must be used. Replace it with the same type as the original.

PHOTOELECTRIC LIGHT CONTROLS

Some electrical/electronic devices that have become very popular, especially in rural and suburban areas, are *automatic yardlights*. They come in all shapes and sizes, such as post-lanterns, floodlights, spotlights, and even mercury-vapor types like those used for street lighting. The mercury-vapor lights can illuminate large areas when they are mounted on high poles. They all use the same kind of control unit—a photoelectric cell that is exposed to the outside light. When this falls below a preset light level, the lamp turns on. The same type of mechanism is used in many cities to control streetlights, electric signs, and similar devices.

Fig. 11-5 shows the schematic of a typical unit. This is one of the smaller types, which is mounted on top of a reflector,

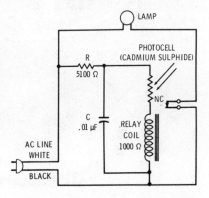

Fig. 11-5. Schematic diagram of a small photoelectric cell. When light falls on the photocell, its resistance goes down and more current flows through the relay; its coil is energized and pulls the contacts open. This extinguishes the lamp.

and uses bulbs with ratings up to 300 watts. Here, the ac current comes in at the top (white) wire, flows through a 5100-ohm resistor (R) and through a cadmium-sulphide cell (abbreviated CdS), then through the relay coil, and back to the line. The CdS cell in this application is a "variable resistor." The arrows denote the fact that the resistance is determined by the amount of *light* which falls on the surface. When it is dark, the cell has a high resistance; when light falls on it, the resistance goes down, allowing more current to flow. The actual control of the lamp bulb is done by the contacts of the sensitive relay. These contacts are normally closed, meaning that when the relay has no current through it, the spring holds the contacts closed and the light is on.

Fig. 11-6. A photoelectric control unit with the cover removed. All parts are exposed for inspection and testing.

When light falls on the photocell, its resistance goes down and more current flows through the relay; its coil is energized and pulls the contacts open, extinguishing the lamp. This gives the device a "fail-safe" operation—if anything goes wrong with the control circuits, the lamp will stay on all the time. Fig. 11-6 shows the photoelectric control unit with cover removed. The relay is at the right, and the rectangular plastic-covered object at the top is the CdS photocell. The flat, light-colored object is the resistor, and the capacitor is alongside it. The reflector can be seen under the unit. The contact points of the relay are at the bottom, and the spring can be seen on top of the coil. In normal operation, a dome-shaped cover is placed over the unit and a small, round window allows light to reach the photocell. Most manufacturers recommend that this be installed so that the window faces north. This keeps the direct rays of the sun from striking the photocell and gives more accurate control of operation.

To check one of these units, replace the lamp with one known to be good. Then cover the photocell window with the palm of your hand; you should be able to hear the relay click. If nothing happens, turn the power off and take off the cover. There will be several hot wires exposed when the cover is removed, and you will probably be standing on a ladder, so do not take any chances. Check the relay contacts. If these are dirty, burned, or pitted, they may not be making good contact. In most of these units, the relay contacts will be easily accessible, as shown in Fig. 11-6. Pull a strip of fine sandpaper between the contacts to clean them and make sure that the spring has enough tension to pull them firmly together. Look for signs of visible damage. If lightning has struck anywhere near the area, there is always the possibility of damage. It will leave definite traces through burned resistors or charred parts and smoked places where the current has flashed across insulation, etc. If this has happened, remove the unit for repairs.

If there are no visible signs of damage, use an insulated tool, like a plastic rod, wooden dowel, etc., and turn the power back on, being *very* careful not to touch any of the exposed terminals. Using the insulated tool, very gently push the relay contacts together. If the lamp lights, then this much is operating properly. Next, cover the photocell with a pad, dark cloth, cardboard, etc. This should make the relay armature move. In this circuit, covering the photocell should open the armature, allowing the contacts to close, and turning the lamp on. If the relay armature does not move, then the unit will have to be removed for an electrical checkup. (Be sure to turn the power off first.) This will require a small volt-ohmmeter because the resistance of the complete circuit must be checked. Check the total resistance across the ac line terminals. All of these resistance measurements must be made with *both* wires disconnected from the ac line. The resistor, as shown in Fig. 11-5, should read 5100 ohms, the relay coil about 1000 ohms, and the photocell between 2000 and about 15,000 ohms, depending on the amount of light falling on it.

Cover the face of the cell and take a resistance reading directly across the terminals. The "dark-reading" should be high. Uncover the cell and let the bench light strike it; the resistance should drop to about 1500 to 2000 ohms. If all of these readings are correct, the unit should work. Most of these units use a small capacitor (C) across the relay coil and photocell as a filter. If this should be shorted, the relay will not work and the 5100-ohm resistor may be burned up as well. Check the total resistance across the capacitor terminals. This should be the sum of the resistances of the photocell and the relay coil, as in Fig. 11-5. For example, if the cell is covered, you should read about 15,000 ohms. If the capacitor is shorted, you may read 100 to 200 ohms or even a dead short (zero resistance). To make a reliable test, disconnect one end of the capacitor and recheck the resistance. You should never read any resistance between the leads of a good capacitor. It should be a completely open circuit. If the capacitor is shorted, remove it and take it to a radio-television shop, they can tell you what value it was by its color code. If they can't determine the value, a $0.01\text{-}\mu\text{F}$ capacitor at 600 working volts is a good compromise value, since it is the most common size found in such circuits.

In the unit shown in Fig. 11-6, you can get at the working parts for replacement by taking the socket off, then the reflector. These are held by screws inside the reflector. The control unit is held in place by two long screws; the heads of these can be seen next to the relay coil. They will not come out from this side; there are two nuts on each screw on the underside. These can be taken off after the socket and reflector have been removed. This uses a printed-circuit type of board, with all of the solder connections on the underside.

Fig. 11-7 shows the schematic of a larger unit. Although it is exactly like the first unit in principle, it has some refinements. It is used to control heavy-duty mercury-vapor lamps like those used for street lighting or for large area lighting in rural areas. This is a plug-in unit; the complete control unit

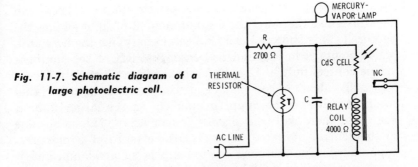

Fig. 11-7. Schematic diagram of a large photoelectric cell.

can be removed by turning it slightly to the left (counterclockwise) and then pulling it up and out of its socket. Fig. 11-8 shows the construction. Note the similarity to the first unit. Relay contacts are larger so that they can handle the heavier currents. A temperature-compensating resistor is mounted across coil and photocell. The "wing-shaped" devices seen at

Fig. 11-8. Shows the construction of a heavy-duty photoelectric control unit.

the right are overlapping Polaroid plastic shutters. These can be adjusted so that only the desired amount of light strikes the photocell. This photocell is a CdS cell exactly like the first unit, but is mounted in a cylindrical case, just left of the shutters.

The control unit in Fig. 11-5 works almost instantly. There is usually about a 1-second delay between the light striking the photocell and the lamp turning on. In the larger unit of Fig. 11-7, there will be a slightly longer delay. This is not due to the control unit, but to the characteristics of a mercury-vapor lamp. The mercury-vapor lamp is an arc lamp, and it takes a second or two for it to build up enough voltage to "strike." This delay will not be noticeable in normal operation, but if there is a violent thunderstorm with fairly constant lightning flashes, you may notice the lamp going off, on, then off again erratically. After a particularly brilliant flash, it may go off and stay off for quite a while. The photocells can be temporarily *blocked* by large amounts of light, just as the human eye can be momentarily blinded. However, this will not damage anything unless the lamp is actually hit by lightning.

SOLID-STATE LIGHT DIMMERS

Solid-state light dimmer switches have become fairly common of late. While these are not repairable, being black boxes, they can be tested. These units use a device called a semiconductor controlled rectifier (SCR), which in effect "chops out" pieces of the incoming ac voltage to reduce the total power applied to the lamp. This, along with its "gating" device, will be completely sealed in a tiny box, small enough to go inside the standard switch boxes in the wall.

If the dimmer unit refuses to turn the lamps on, the first thing that should be checked is the lamps themselves. If these are good, then take the cover plate off and check for ac voltage at the terminals of the dimmer unit. If there is voltage going into the unit but none coming out at any setting of the dimmer control, the unit is bad. It will have to be replaced.

Being semiconductors, these units can be damaged by lightning striking nearby. The most common damage is a short. If this happens, the lamps will refuse to dim; when they are switched on, they'll stay at full brightness at all times, at all settings of the dim control. If the lamps start to dim normally, then go out entirely at a certain setting, the control itself is defective. Once again, the whole unit will have to be replaced.

Some of the lower-priced or earlier versions will cause interference to nearby radio and tv sets. To be sure that the dimmer is the cause of the interference, just turn the light off; if the interference disappears, the dimmer is causing it. Some interference can be cleared up by connecting a pair of small bypass capacitors (.01 μF at 600 working volts, ceramic type) across the ac output line from the dimmer. Be SURE that the power is turned OFF before you try this!

Chapter 12

Miscellaneous Repair Techniques

A lot of the "little things" often get left out of a book like this simply because they don't fall into a definite category. These are the little tricks that professional appliance repairmen use to make the job faster and easier. We'll discuss some of these work-savers in this chapter.

REPAIRING BROKEN APPLIANCE CASES

The cases and housings of modern appliances are made of one of two materials—sheet metal or molded plastic. In some, a combination of the two is used. By the law of averages, a lot of these are dropped or knocked off tables, breaking the cases. Most of these can be repaired without too much trouble. The early plastic cases had a tendency to shatter like glass. The newer cases are made of high-impact-type plastics, which will crack but normally won't shatter.

Metal cases will be mostly thin sheet steel or aluminum stamped into the desired shape. Although these types of cases will dent or bend, they are hard to break. Dents in aluminum or thin sheet steel can be hammered out, using a very light hammer and extreme care. Steel cases may be soldered if they crack. Aluminum may be soldered by using aluminum solder and a very clean iron, but not as easily as steel and similar metals.

Some units may have cases made of a cast-metal alloy, known contemptuously to old-time machinists as pot metal or pewter, etc. This doesn't have much strength, and it is almost impossible to solder. (Solder won't stick to it.) Don't give up; there *is* a way to repair them, and it is discussed later in this chapter.

PLASTIC CASES

Plastics used in appliances can be divided into two groups. The first group is the "thermoplastic" type, meaning that after the material has been molded, it can be softened by heating. The other group is the "thermosetting" type. After this kind of plastic is molded and set, the application of heat won't soften it at all. However, thermosetting plastics can be repaired by using epoxy cement, which is discussed later in this chapter.

To find out which kind of plastic you are working with, touch the tip of a hot soldering iron to a point on the inside of the case. If the material melts, it's a thermoplastic. You can repair cracks in cases made of this type of material by running the tip of the hot soldering iron along the crack. This melts the plastic, letting it flow back together. The case should be clamped or held so that it can't move for a couple minutes in order to set the plastic. This can be done with standard clamps or by snapping rubber bands around the sides of the housing. Little pressure is needed—only enough to keep the break from pulling apart until the repair sets.

Many plastic cases can be cemented back together, using common household cement, airplane glue, etc. To find out if this type of cement will hold, put a drop of it on a spot inside the case. Wipe if off in about 30 seconds and see if it has attacked the surface, leaving it roughened. If so, the cement will match the type of plastic used and make a strong joint. If the cement wipes off cleanly, leaving no trace, it may or may not hold the repaired joint (try another cement).

If it matches, pry the end of the crack open just a little and slip a match or toothpick between the ends to keep it open. Now, run a small bead of the cement along the crack, squeezing the tube lightly. Work the cement inside the crack with a toothpick. Next, take the toothpick out of the end of the case and let the sides snap back together. Clamp or tie it, if necessary, to hold the sides of the break together snugly. If you're lucky, the joint will fit so tightly that the resultant seam won't even be visible from the outside. Last, before setting the case aside to dry, wipe any excess cement off the outside with a clean cloth. It'll be easier to get off before it dries. If any cement squeezes out inside the case, leave it; it won't be seen. Let the cement dry for at least 8 hours to make sure that it sets perfectly.

REPAIRING THE TOUGH ONES

Now for those tough jobs that I mentioned. There is a type of cement that could almost be called "universal." It will bond to almost any material—wood, metal, plastic, etc., and it has tremendous strength when dry and cured. This is called an "epoxy-resin" cement, epoxy for short. The best kind is the two-compound type. You'll get two small tubes; one is the resin, the other a "hardener" compound. The two are mixed together just before use. There are single compounds similar to this that are already mixed, but some of these have a limited shelf life and do not have the strength of the two-compound variety.

To use epoxy cement properly, clean the joint thoroughly. Wash off all traces of oil, dirt, paint, grease, etc. If necessary, scrape the surface with a sharp knife blade, or sand it. Now, get a small piece of scrap glass or one of those little aluminum dishes that frozen food comes in. (This must also be clean, of course!) Squeeze one drop of the resin onto this surface. Now, squeeze one drop of the hardener onto the surface. One drop is clear, the other golden yellow. Using the end of a wooden match or a small screwdriver, thoroughly mix the two together. Keep stirring until the whole drop is a clear amber color or slightly creamy. Now it's ready to use.

Use the same application method as with other cements. Open the crack and put a toothpick in it, etc. Using the tip of the small screwdriver, work the epoxy cement well along the crack until the whole length is covered. (After a little practice, you'll know how big a drop of cement to mix up. It takes a surprisingly small amount of this stuff to patch even a good-sized break!) Now, take the block out and hold the sides of the crack together. Use a clamp or rubber bands to keep the pieces in place. Very little pressure is needed.

Turn the case over and wipe the epoxy off the outside. Do it now because after the epoxy sets, you'll have a hard time getting it off! Epoxy cement sets fairly rapidly. However, for maximum strength, let the joint set at least overnight or about 8 hours. You will be surprised at the strength of the repair; the cracked place is often stronger than the rest of the case.

If the case is thin and hard to hold, you can make up little braces or "gussets"; these can be cemented across the crack at different points for added strength. The braces can be cut out of sheet tin, thin stiff plastic, or any suitable material. Be sure that they will not interfere with the closing of the case or any of the machinery!

Finally, after you're through making a joint with epoxy, clean up all tools used, such as the screwdriver. If you let the epoxy set on them, you'll have trouble getting it off. The mixing glass can be wiped off and put up for the next time. If you use the little aluminum pans, throw them away; there are always enough of these around the modern kitchen!

If you have a really bad break, you may have to take drastic measures. You can make up small bracing plates out of sheet tin, aluminum, etc., bending them at right angles to fit inside places on the case needing reinforcement. Cement the braces in place. Or, as an alternate method, you can carefully drill at least four small holes in the case so that they will hit the corners of the brace plate. If you have a variable-speed drill, use a slow speed. If not, feed the bit very slowly into the soft plastic to keep from overheating and melting it. After these holes have been made, set the brace plate in position inside the case. Mark through the holes with a soft lead pencil. Now, drill *smaller* holes through the plate at these points.

To fasten the plate, get some self-tapping or sheet-metal screws. The panhead types are best for this; they have wide oval heads to give better hold on plastic or sheet metal. Get a screw that will just start into the holes in the *plate,* but will pass through the holes in the plastic case without cutting threads. About a No. 6 or No. 8 screw would be the best size. Set the plate in position and run the screws through the holes; they'll cut their own threads in the metal. For added strength, you can coat the underside of the plate with cement.

BROKEN STUDS

A great many appliances are held together by self-tapping screws, which go through holes in one half of the case and then into small molded studs on the other half. The studs are hollow; the mounting screws cut their own threads in the soft plastic. The studs often break off if the appliance is dropped. If the whole stud breaks off at its base, it can be put back with epoxy cement. Some times the stud will split down the middle so that the screws won't hold. This can be repaired with the epoxy cement; clamp the broken halves together neatly. It's usually a good idea to get the screw that fits in the stud, put a drop of oil on its threads, and run it down almost to the bottom in the original threads. This will keep any excess epoxy from getting inside and clogging the threads. If this happens, the stud will split again the first time the screw is run down into it! The oil will keep the epoxy from sticking to the screw threads, and it can be taken out after the epoxy has cured and set.

BOLTS, NUTS, AND SCREWS

One of the little things that can give you a lot of trouble is the "fastenings"; that is, the bolts, nuts, and screws that hold the appliances together. To repair them, we have to take the fastenings out, and this is often the hardest part of the whole job!

The secret to easily taking out the fasteners is using the proper *tools*. You'll find at least four different types of screws used. The difference lies in the heads. The plain slotted type used to be almost universally used. This is "A" in Fig. 12-1. Slotted types come in all sizes. The secret of getting them out without damage is the size of screwdriver you use and its

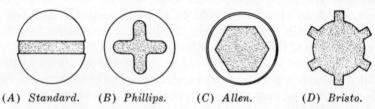

(A) *Standard.*   (B) *Phillips.*   (C) *Allen.*   (D) *Bristo.*

Fig. 12-1. Some popular types of screw heads used in small appliances.

sharpness. For the best results, always pick a screwdriver that will fit in the slot snugly, without any slack. If the screwdriver is too small, the edges of the bit will climb up the sides of the slot and damage it. After a couple of tries with a screwdriver that is too small, the slot will be so badly burred that you may never get the screw out.

At "B" in Fig. 12-1, you see a type that is becoming popular with manufacturers (not with the technicians and handymen who have to take them out). These screws can be set with power-driven tools faster than the slotted types! The first of

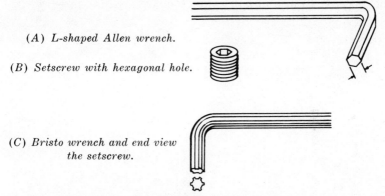

(A) L-shaped Allen wrench.

(B) Setscrew with hexagonal hole.

(C) Bristo wrench and end view the setscrew.

Fig. 12-2. Allen and Bristo wrenches and setscrews.

these screws was called a Phillips screw, after its inventor. You will find other screws, which could all be lumped together under the common term, "cross-slot" screws; the screwdrivers are called "cross-point" types. Here again, the secret of working easily with these is to be sure that the screwdriver *fits* snugly into the slots. If the head is either too big or too small, it will burr the slots, causing a smooth-sided conical pit! Be sure that the head will "bottom" in the slot.

Many of the cross-point screws found in imported units have a slot that is not as *deep* as the United States standard types. Standard screwdrivers won't grip the slots because the screwdriver point is too long. To make a standard screwdriver work better with the screws on imported units, grind a *tiny bit* of the sharp tip off. This will let the edges get a better "bite," and the shallow-slot screws will loosen up.

A third type of screw is called an Allen screw (Fig. 12-1C). It has a hexagonal hole in the end and is used mainly as a setscrew. Special wrenches which are little L-shaped bits of very tough steel, must be used. The wrench is slipped inside the hexagonal hole and turned. A variation of the Allen screw has splines instead of a hexagonal shape. It is called a Bristo screw (Fig. 12-1D). A Bristo and an Allen wrench are shown in Fig. 12-2. These wrenches are available in kits of many different sizes at hardware stores, auto supply stores, etc. The small sizes will be the only ones you need for average appliance work. The wrenches come in little plastic pouches. Use these pouches to keep the wrenches together; they're so small that they're easy to lose in a crowded toolbox.

Chapter **13**

Appliance Servicing

Whether you want to service your own appliances to save time and money, or whether you want to go into appliance service as a part-time or even full-time job, you'll get along much more easily if you have the right tools. There are certain appliances that you won't even be able to take apart at all, unless you have the proper tool! For the home handyman, you might use your regular tools until you run into a unit needing a special one. Then, go buy that tool, and you'll have it for the next project! After a few jobs like this, you'll be all set. There aren't really too many different types.

If you're going into appliance servicing as a business, tools are an absolute necessity. The right tool saves time, and time is money. The first part of this chapter discusses various uses for specific types of tools and then takes up the important subject of where and how to get replacement parts.

TIMESAVING TOOLS

Fig. 13-1 shows a group of really handy tools—screw-holding screwdrivers. You're going to find a lot of places where you need three hands, and these are a dandy "third hand"; they hold the screw while you hold the pieces in place with the other hand. There are two basic types, the outside-clip and the inside-grip. The first is used on both slot and Phillips-head screws. The inside-grip type is a special version; it can be used in places where the bulkier outside-clip type won't go.

An inside-grip holder is shown at the extreme right of Fig. 13-1. These are made in several sizes; this one will hold the common sizes found in most appliances, from a No. 6 to a No. 10. The end of the blade is split, and as the handle is pushed down, the central portion of the blade turns, wedging the split ends of the blade against the sides of the slot. The

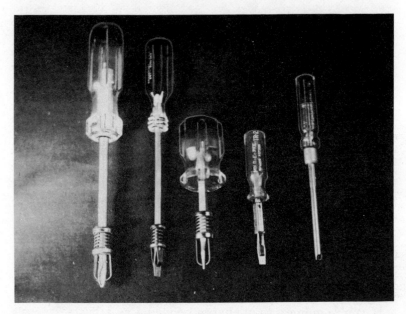

Fig. 13-1. Some screw-holding screwdrivers. At the extreme left is the outside-clip type for Phillips screws. The inside grip at the extreme right, being no bigger than the screw, will fit into tight places which are often too snug for the outside-clip type.

major advantage of this type of driver is that it is no bigger than the screw; if the screw can go into the available space, so can the holder. On the other hand, the outside-clip type is sometimes too big to fit into a narrow space.

Fig. 13-2 shows another group of handy tools, called nut holders. They are exactly like standard hex-nut drivers, except the socket is split lengthwise and is slightly larger than the size marked. It is slipped over the hex-head bolt or nut, and a sliding collar wedges the two halves together, gripping the nut or bolt very tightly. One distinct advantage of the nut holder is its strength. Because of its heavily constructed collar and socket, it will tighten nuts and bolts almost as snugly as a standard socket wrench.

The smaller wrench in Fig. 13-2 has a tiny permanent magnet inside the socket. A spring-loaded plastic shaft extending through the handle is used to push small nuts out of the wrench

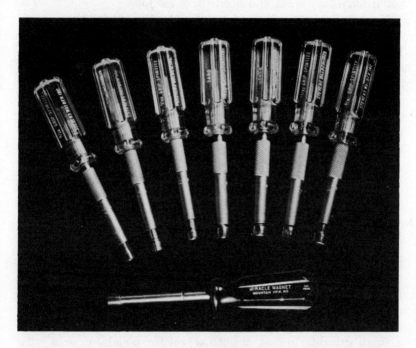

Fig. 13-2. A group of nut holders. The sliding collar holds the bolt or nut in place until inserted. The smaller wrench at the bottom of the picture has a small permanent magnet inside the socket, and the plastic shaft is spring-loaded so the bolts can be pushed out of the socket.

after removal, or to hold short bolts far enough down in it for them to start. Its only disadvantage is its inability to hold nonmagnetic nuts or bolts, such as the small brass nuts used on some appliances.

Small open-end and box-end wrenches are often useful in appliance work, especially where there isn't enough clearance above the nut to allow use of a nut driver. These wrenches can be purchased separately or in sets at auto supply stores—just ask for ignition wrenches. Buy the type with broached sockets, rather than the stamped-out types which don't last as long.

You'll probably find use for several small punches and chisels, also available at auto supply stores in a large assortment of shapes and sizes. It's best to wait until you've done a few jobs before buying any tools, and as you need, say, a certain size of punch or chisel, then buy one. In only a short while you'll have just what you need for most jobs.

You probably won't need a full set of taps and dies, since most appliances use only a few popular sizes such as 8/32 or 10/32. The increasing use of the self-tapping or *sheet-metal* screw has eliminated much of the tedious tapping and threading formerly required.

A small tapered hand reamer, from ⅛ to ½ or ⅝ inch in size, can be very useful. It is available from mail-order and plumbing supply houses, and comes in two types—one for use in a hand brace like carpenters use and the other with a T-shaped handle for hand use.

POWER TOOLS

Power tools such as a drill press or lathe are seldom essential, although there are a few occasions when they come in handy. However, a ¼-inch electric drill with its various attachments can be used for a multitude of appliance repair jobs. A complete set of high-grade twist drills is almost a necessity. However, drilling holes isn't all a drill can do; clamped in a vise, it can be used to turn an arbor that will hold a small grinding wheel, a cloth wheel for polishing, or a wire wheel (a wire brush, sometimes called a scratch wheel) for cleaning and buffing. For such jobs, this handy tool can save many hours of tedious hand work. Some manufacturers have kits like the one in Fig. 13-3, which include the drill motor with a standard chuck, plus attachments for buffing, sanding, and even sawing.

A most useful addition to your tool chest is a hand grinder, which generally includes an assortment of tiny grinding wheels, burrs much like those used by dentists, etc. This is a very handy tool for working in tight places—for example, for grinding off the ends of rivets in places where the larger drill does not reach. The small burrs will do a good job of cleaning small metal parts, grinding off nicks, straightening edges, and the like. They can also be used to ream out a hole when it is too small for the bolt.

Sanding discs, grinding wheels, burrs, and even drill bits can be purchased at auto supply and similar stores. In fact, your dentist may be glad to give you some discarded burrs and bits, which are too dull for his work but can still be highly useful to you.

Fig. 13-3. A typical ¼-inch drill set with attachments for buffing, sanding, and sawing, as well as drilling.

A small- to medium-sized vise, especially one with a rotating base, is a very handy item. This allows you to turn the job to the most convenient angle as you work. Some sort of anvil is also useful. A piece of old iron fastened securely to the bench makes a good one. Or a piece of heavy angle iron 1½ to 2 feet long, turned over the edge of the bench and fastened down with bolts or screws, will serve as a handy anvil and also as a backing for punching rivets or similar jobs.

By drilling different-sized holes in the iron, you can use it and a punch to remove rivets. Set the rivet in the hole closest in size to that of the rivet head. Then use a pin punch with a flat end exactly the size of the rivet shank to drive the rivet through the metal. Never use a center or pointed punch; it will expand the shank of the rivet and thus enlarge the hole in the sheet metal. This makes it necessary to replace the old rivet with a larger one, which can be very unsightly.

When replacing rivets, use only a flat-headed punch or a smooth-faced hammer. To peen the end of a rivet properly, use a series of light taps rather than a few heavy swats for a much better looking and more durable job. Use the same method when you must resort to a flat-end punch to reach a rivet— light taps until the rivet shank is peened over and held securely.

CHEMICAL AIDS

Various chemical products will be very useful for cleaning contacts, cementing parts, insulating wiring, etc. Be careful, though, not to use acetates and acrylates, which are flammable, around very hot parts of an appliance.

Penetrating oils and rust solvents are especially useful in most appliances, since one of your worst headaches is rusted or corroded nuts and bolts that won't come out. Chemical rust solvents are a great help because most nuts and bolts are so small and are made from such comparatively delicate materials (cast aluminum housings, sheet-metal parts, etc.) that you can't use force to loosen them for fear of damaging the appliance.

When you run into a balky nut or bolt, apply the chemical solvent (sold under such trade names as Rust-Off, Liquid Wrench, Nut-Buster, etc.) and let it stand overnight. The rusty nut or bolt will be much more likely to come loose.

WHEN CHEMICALS WON'T WORK

A few special tricks will be helpful when a chemical solvent won't loosen the nut or bolt. Then mechanical methods can be tried, but you'll have to be very careful. If the screw has a standard slot, be sure the screwdriver is sharpened to the correct shape and that it fits the slot. For best results, the screwdriver must be ground as shown in Fig. 13-4A. If the angle is too short (Fig. 13-4B) or if the screwdriver is ground too sharp (Fig. 13-4C), the blade will ride up out of the slot and round off the edges, making it almost impossible to remove the screw. If someone else has already rounded off the screw, throw it away. Never re-use a badly damaged screw or bolt; you're just piling up trouble for the next guy—who just might be you!

(A) *The correct way—a long, gentle angle, an exactly square tip, and sharp edges.*

(B) *The tip is too blunt—it will "ride up" out of the slot and ruin the screw.*

(C) *Fine for chisels, but not for screwdrivers! It, too, will jump out of the slot and mutilate the screw head.*

Fig. 13-4. How, and how not, to grind the tip of a screwdriver.

Damaged screw slots can sometimes be sharpened enough for the screw to be removed. A set of pattern files is very helpful, or use the sanding disc on a hand grinder. If the screw head is inaccessible with the file or hand grinder, grind a screwdriver to the exact size, place it in the slot, and tap it with a hammer. This will sometimes reshape the slot enough to allow removal of the screw.

When its head is broken completely off or when it's so badly damaged that normal removal is impossible, the screw or bolt must be drilled out. A screw extractor—a specially-shaped device with a left-handed thread—is useful here. A hole is drilled through the top of the screw or bolt, and the extractor is screwed into it. As the extractor is turned, its left-handed thread forces it down into the hole, so that the bolt can be turned with it and thus be extracted.

If an extractor is not available or if space prevents its use, select a bit slightly smaller in diameter than the bolt shank. Carefully center-punch the end of the broken bolt and drill straight down into the shank. Correctly done, this will cut out all of the jammed bolt except part of its threads; yet the threads in the hole will be almost undamaged if you're careful. The hole can be rethreaded if damaged by the bit. When a nut and bolt are used and the hole is not threaded, the head of the bolt can be chiseled or ground off and the shank driven through the hole with a flat-ended punch.

PARTS PROCUREMENT

One of the biggest problems in appliance servicing is procurement of replacement parts. Unlike many other devices, such as radio and tv sets, most appliance replacement parts will fit only a few makes and sometimes only one. However, the situation is not completely impossible.

In most large cities there are several appliance-parts supply houses within easy reach. Often, in medium-sized cities, major manufacturers or independent suppliers have set up branch offices where you can buy locally. In small towns, however, because no local source of supply is usually available, you will probably have to depend on mail-order service. Few locations are more than 100 miles from an appliance parts distributor; in fact, there is usually a choice of four or five within this range.

The local dealer carrying this brand of appliance will probably have a small stock of replacement parts. If he doesn't, he can tell you where the state distributor for this make is located. This is usually in the state capital or the largest city. Distributors often have branch parts depots in medium to large cities.

There are also quite a few specialized appliance parts wholesalers all over the country. These companies carry exact-duplicate parts for many makes and universal parts, such as line cords, heating elements, and similar things. In a lot of cases, the independent parts wholesaler can give you quicker service than the state distributor for a particular make! To get the correct part from a manufacturer, you must have *his* stock number for it, or the order will often be sent back, saying "no such part"! The independent parts wholesalers issue very comprehensive catalogues, which are invaluable as a source of reference material. Get as many as you can, and keep them filed. These are usually sent free or for a small charge refunded on your first order.

If you're going into the business, contact other appliance repair shops in your area and find out where they have the best luck in getting replacement parts. You may find that in your community the factory distributor gives the best service. This service has been vastly improved over the last few years! A lot of makers now have toll-free *hot lines*, where parts orders can be telephoned in without charge.

Another problem for out-of-town purchases is transportation. Check the mail schedules from the nearest cities. Also check the UPS schedules for areas served by United Parcel Service. Find out when the mail is sent out from the city in question. For example, if there is a mail shipment leaving the city at 10:00 A.M., you can telephone an order in at 9:00 A.M. and get it the same day. Another fast transportation service is the bus line. The same methods apply; find out when busses leave the city that you are ordering the part from, and order by telephone. Distance is often unimportant. Quite often, a city farther away geographically will be the place offering the quickest service, due to transportation routes, arrivals and departure schedules of busses and mail trucks, and so on. Make yourself up a little chart showing the latest times you can telephone in an order and still get same-day delivery of parts.

If a part is unobtainable from any nearby sources, you will have to order directly from the factory, and you can count on a delay of several days or even weeks for delivery. For emergency repairs where cost is a minor item, telephoning the factory service manager and requesting shipment by Air Express will usually get you quicker service than ordering by letter. Often a telegram will work. For the same rate as a day letter, night letters allow you to use more words and hence longer descriptions of the part, yet with only a few hours' lag in delivery time.

How many parts to stock is determined by your volume of appliance business and the nearness of suppliers. Of course, you should stock as many as possible, in order not to waste time running after parts—but within limits. Because of rapid obsolescence and the lack of interchangeability, you can easily accumulate a large and expensive collection of "dogs." The best way for the first few months is to carry only the minimum stock of parts and note which ones you use most. Then a small stock of these can be laid in. Later, as your business grows, others can be added. Of course, universal parts such as line cords, appliance plugs, and the like can be purchased immediately and in fairly large quantities, since all appliances use them.

One method of obtaining fairly rapid delivery of parts if you plan to engage heavily in the appliance business, is to contact as many well-known manufacturers as possible and ask for an appointment as a factory-authorized service station for their line. If you secure a go-ahead, make the rounds of all appliance dealers within your trade area and let them know you now have this authorization. Many will gladly give you all their warranty replacement work, and in this way you can build up your volume of appliance business to the point where it will be more worth your while to carry an adequate stock of replacement parts.

One last word about parts procurement: Customers are often impatient to have an appliance repaired. For some reason, they don't mind waiting a reasonable length of time, *as long as you deliver when promised!* But if they have to wait one more day, you're in deep trouble! Customers in smaller towns don't seem to be as demanding as those in larger cities; they're accustomed to waiting and as a rule are quite patient. For the "can't wait" customer who must have the job done immediately, tell him or her that you'll be very happy to oblige —but there will be a small extra charge for long-distance telephone calls, bus charges, etc. Tell him how much—he may change his mind and give you all the time you need.

Glossary

A

Armature—That portion of a motor (the rotating member) that includes the main current-carrying winding.

Asbestos—A fibrous fireproof material used in heater cords and in other applications where excessive heat may present a fire hazard.

Auxiliary Switch—A switch used to support another one in the performance of a desired function.

B

Bimetal Blade—A blade used primarily in thermostats. It is comprised of two dissimilar metals, one having a high expansion rate as it is heated and the other a low expansion rate.

Brick—A molded ceramic form on which the heating element of an appliance is mounted. Sometimes the element is embedded in the brick.

Brush—A carbon or metal block that provides electrical contact with the rotating member of an electrical device.

Brush Chatter—A condition that exists when the commutator on a motor armature is out of round or has a rough or uneven surface, causing the brushes to bounce as the armature rotates.

Bypass Capacitor—A component used in a number of motor-operated household appliances to reduce arcing and/or to suppress noise which could interfere with radio and tv reception.

C

Cam—A rotating or sliding lever used to give complicated and precisely timed movements in a machine or engine.

Capacitor—A component comprised of two conductors separated by an insulating material known as the dielectric.

Centrifugal Speed Regulator—A device which governs the speed of a motor by utilizing the force that tends to impel an object outward from its center of rotation.

Ceramic—A nonconducting material commonly used as a mounting for heating elements or in feedthrough insulators, etc.

Commutator—That portion of an armature comprised of copper segments against which the brushes make contact.

Conductor—A material that offers little or no opposition to the flow of electric current.

Contacts—Two circular pieces of hardened steel mounted on supporting conductors, used to provide intermittent connection between circuits or between different parts of the same circuit.

Continuity—The property of having a continuous dc electrical path.

Current Drain—The amount of current drawn from a source.

E

Eccentric Cam—A cam having unequal radii. (See *Cam*.)

Electromagnetic Field—A combination of electric and magnetic fields produced by the flow of electric current through a wire or coil.

Electromechanical Device—A device that is both mechanical and electrical, such as an automatic toaster.

F

Feedthrough Insulator—A tubular insulator (usually made of ceramic) inserted into a hole through which a conductor must pass. It is used to keep the conductor from shorting against the sides of the hole.

Field Coil—The coils that produce the magnetic field in a motor.

G

Grommet—An insulating washer, usually made of rubber or plastic, inserted into a metal hole to prevent a wire or cable from scraping against the sides of the hole.

Ground—The neutral, or low, side of a power line or an appliance. In the latter, the frame is considered ground.

Growler—An electromagnetic device used for locating defective coils in an armature. It derives its name from the growling noise produced as the armature is rotated within its jaws.

H

Heater Cord—A heavy-duty two-conductor cord designed primarily for home appliances requiring large amounts of power.

Heating Element—A low-resistance wire which becomes very hot as a result of its opposition to current flowing through it.

High-Resistance Connection—A connection that offers a large opposition to the flow of electric current. This can be caused by a connection being loose, corroded, rusted, etc.

Housing—A protective device which surrounds the working components of a motor, appliance, etc.

I

Ignition Wrenches—Small open or box-end wrenches used primarily for working on ignition systems, radios, etc.

Insulation—A nonconducting material used to prevent a current from taking undesired paths as it flows through a conductor.

Interlock Plug—A plug that automatically becomes disconnected from the circuit when disassembly of a device is begun.

K

Kilowatt—1000 watts.

L

Laminated—Being made up of layers, such as the laminated core of a coil.
Line Cord—A two-conductor wire terminated with a two-prong plug, used for connecting to a wall outlet.

M

Magnetic Contacts—A set of contacts that are snapped together by magnetic attraction when a specified distance apart. They prevent arcing that would otherwise occur if the contacts were to come together slowly.
Magnetic Field—The immediate area, around a magnet or a current-carrying conductor or coil, where magnetic lines of force exist.
Mechanism—In a device, the mechanical parts needed to perform its intended function.
Mica—A material with excellent insulating and heat-resisting properties. Mica insulating washers are often used around and under electrical terminals on household appliances.

N

Neon Lamp—A small neon-filled lamp used as an indicating device on a number of appliances. Applying a voltage of the correct value causes the gas within the lamp to glow.

O

Ohm—The unit of resistance.
Ohmmeter—An instrument used to measure resistance.
Ohm's Law Formula—The formula that expresses the relationship between voltage, current, and resistance—for example $I = E \div R$.
Open—A circuit or component in which the electrical path is no longer continuous.
Oven Thermometer—A special thermometer used to check high temperatures in an oven, rotisserie, etc.

P

Pattern File—A small fine-toothed file.
Permanent Magnet—A piece of metal that retains its magnetism after the magnetizing force has been removed.
Phillips Screw—A screw with a + instead of a slot in the head.
"Pigtail"—A braided copper wire fastened to the end of a brush to provide contact between the brush and the rest of the circuit.

R

Receptacle—A socket or other outlet into which a plug can be inserted to make electrical contact.
Resistance Wire—A wire that becomes very hot due to its high opposition to the flow of electrical current. It is used principally as a heating element in household appliances.

Revolution—One complete turn around an axis.

Rivet—A soft metal pin or bolt used to untie two or more pieces of metal.

Rotary Switch—A switch having its contacts mounted in a circle.

S

Safetied Splice—A splice that has been secured with additional material to ensure maximum strength and thus safety.

Screw Extractor—A device used for removing "frozen" or broken screws.

Self-Tapping Screw—A tapered screw, made of hard metal, that forms its own threads as it is driven into a material.

Setscrew—A screw having a hexagonal hole through its center in place of a head. A hexagonal L-shaped tool known as an Allen wrench is inserted in the hole to loosen or tighten the screw.

Silicone Grease—A grease with a higher-than-normal melting point.

Spit—A slender rod with prongs used for holding meat over a fire.

Splice—A joint between two conductors that has mechanical strength as well as electrical conductivity.

Strain Relief—A device used to grip the line cord in order to keep strain off the electrical connections.

SV Cord—A cord comprised of two rubber-insulated conductors surrounded by a fiber lay and covered with heavy rubber or plastic.

Synchronous Motor—A motor that operates on the principle of magnetic repulsion and attraction. It requires no brushes or commutators.

T

Thermostat—A device that automatically regulates the temperature produced by a heating element. (Also see *Bimetal Blade.*)

Timer—A device that can be set to control a particular operation for a predetermined length of time.

U

Underwriter's Code—A set of electrical standards established by a group of fire and casualty insurance companies, and now adopted as a legal requirement by many cities.

V

Voltage Frequency—The number of cycles an ac voltage goes through during one second.

Voltmeter—A meter used to measure potential difference (voltage).

W

Watt—A unit of electrical power.

Wattmeter—A meter used to measure electrical power.

Wire Nut—A tapered plastic or ceramic nut that is screwed down onto a wire splice to hold it securely.

Worm Gear—A cylindrical gear with grooves similar to bolt threads.

Z

Zip Cord—A stranded two-conductor wire covered with rubber or plastic and having a groove down the center to permit easy separation.

Index

A

Aids, chemical, 150
Appliance(s)
  beauty-care, 118-121
  cases, repairing broken, 138-139
  connectors, 34-36
  dual-heat, 66, 68
Automatic toasters, servicing, 90-91

B

Ballast, 129
Basic electrical tests, 18-21
Beauty-care appliances, 118-121
Blankets, 122-125
Bolts, 142-144
Bottle warmers, 92-93
Broken
  appliance cases, repairing, 138-139
  studs, 142

C

Cable, three-wire, 23
Calibrated thermostats, 72-74
Cases
  broken appliances, repairing, 138-139
  plastic, 139-140
Cement, 120, 140-141
Checking
  and repair, 120
  line cords, 31-32
Chemical aids, 150
Cleaning, switch, 15
Coffee makers, 68-69
Combination toaster and table oven, 103-106
Connections, 113-114
Connectors, appliance, 34-36
Continuity, 19
Controlling heat, 40-41
Controls, photoelectric light, 131-136
Cooker
  fondue, 73
  hot-dog, 91-92
Cord(s)
  attachments, 32-34
  heater, 23
  line, 21
  POSJ, 22
  SV, 22
  types of, 21-22
Curlers, hair, 118

D

Deep-fat fryer, 63-64
Dimmers, solid-state light, 136-137

Disassembly, 103-106, 120-121
Dual-heat appliances, 66, 68

E

Electric griddles, 60
Electrical
  testing, 12-15
  tests, basic, 18-21
Element(s)
  heating, 51-54
  replacement, 113
Epoxy-resin cement, 140-141

F

Fan motors, 117-118
Fasteners, 38
Files, pattern, 91
Fluorescent lights, 129-131
Fondue cooker, 73

G

Glossary, 155-158
Griddles, electric, 60
Grounds, testing for, 14-15

H

Hair
  curlers, 118
  setters, 119-120
Heat, controlling, 40-41
Heater
  cord, 23
  repairs, 110-118
Heating
  element, 51-54
    repairing, 43-45
    replacement, 69-71
    testing, 43-45
  pads, 125
Hot-dog cooker, 91-92

I

Irons
  steam, 76, 78
    dry/spray, 106-109
    spray, 78, 80

L

Lamps, three-way, 126-129
Light(s)
  controls, photoelectric, 131-136
  dimmers, solid-state, 136-137
  fluorescent, 129-131

Line
  attachments, 21
  cords, 21
    checking, 31-32
    three-wire, 10-11
  plugs, 21
    three-wire, 10-11
Lubricants, 91

M

Motors, 54-56
  fan, 117-118

N

Nuts, 142-144

O

Ohmmeter, testing with, 19-21

P

Pads, heating, 125
Parts procurement, 152-154
Pattern files, 91
Percolator, 96-98
Photoelectric light controls, 131-136
Plastic cases, 139-140
Plugs, 29-30
POSJ cord, 22
Power tools, 148-150
Precautions, safety, 8-9
Procurement, parts, 152-154

R

Receptacles, three-wire, 10-11
Repair, and checking, 120
Repairing
  broken appliance cases, 138-139
  heating elements, 43-45
Repairs, 80
  heater, 110-118
Replacement
  elements, 113
  heating elements, 69-71
  switch, 15
Rotisseries, 50-56

S

Safety
  ground, 10-11
  precautions, 8-9
Screws, 142-144
Self-lowering toasters, 87-90
Servicing, 58, 60
  automatic toasters, 90-91
Setters, hair, 119-120
Skillets, 57
Solid-state light dimmers, 136-137
Splicing sleeves, 44
Starter, 129

Steam
  dry/spray iron, 106-109
  irons, 76, 78
  spray irons, 78, 80
Strain reliefs, 32-34
Studs, broken, 142
SV cord, 22
Switch, 54, 117
  cleaning, 15
  replacement, 15

T

Table oven and toaster, combination, 103-106
Techniques, testing, 11
Test(s)
  basic electrical, 18-21
  lamps, using, 13
Testing, 15-18
  electrical, 12-15
  for grounds, 14-15
  heating elements, 43-45
  techniques, 11
  with ohmmeter, 19-21
Thermostats, 54, 72, 116
  calibrated, 72-74
Three
  way lamps, 126-129
  wire cable, 23
    line cords, 10-11
    plugs, 10-11
    receptacles, 10-11
Timer, 51
Timesaving tools, 145-148
Toaster(s), 99-103
  and table oven, combination, 103-106
  automatic, servicing, 90-91
  self-lowering, 87-90
Tools, 15-18
  power, 148-150
  timesaving, 145-148
Troubleshooting, 106
Types of cords, 21-22

U

Universal heating element, 45
Using test lamps, 13

V

Vaporizers, 93-94

W

Waffle irons, 60-62
Warmers, bottle, 92-93
Warming plates, 62
When chemicals won't work, 150-152
Wire
  nuts, 38
  sizes, 25-29

Z

Zip cord, 22